Getting Back at Dad

GETTING BACK AT DAD

Deanne Stillman

WIDEVIEW
BOOKS

Manufactured in the United States of America.
FIRST EDITION

Library of Congress Cataloging in Publication Data
Stillman, Deanne.
    Getting back at dad.
      I. Title.
PN6162.S85   814'.54   81-50313
ISBN 0-87223-725-7 (pbk.)   AACR2

Wideview Books/A Division of PEI Books, Inc.

"The Crybabies of 'Sixty Minutes,'" "God, Man and Johnny Carson,"
"Ohio: It's Between Indiana and Pennsylvania," and "The Etiquette of
Getting High" (as "Dope Etiquette") originally appeared in *High Times*
magazine. "Pimento" and "The Feminish Dictionary" originally appeared
in *Titters*, "How to Become a Rock Critic in Seven Easy Lessons" and
"Do You Type in the Nude?" (as "You Volunteer Your Love and Flesh")
originally appeared in *More* magazine. "The Good, The Bad, The Don't-
You-Ever-Call-Him Ugly" was first published in *The Daily News*. "Lunch
at Lamston's" appeared first in *Junk Food*.

Illustrations for "Ann Van Brothers Talks to Teens" are by Mary Wil-
shire, illustrations for "Liquid Cash" by Ken Weiner.

To Rex Weiner,

the fastest editor in the East

Acknowledgments

With very special thanks to Cameron Barry, Anne Beatts, Ruth Charny, Gail Hochman, Anne Kostick, Lee Mason, Mom, Robin Rue, Ellen Sherman, George Solomon, Nancy Stillman, and Rosie Stillman.

Contents

GREAT WRITERS

THAT'S ENTERTAINMENT

THIS BIG WORLD OF OURS

"Life is funny, oh dear, oh dear."
                    —REBECCA COHEN

"Honk if you know the difference between parody and satire."
                    —ANON.

Getting Back at Dad

Introduction:

Getting Back at Dad,

or Why I Write

When asked why they write, some writers won't tell. "My work speaks for itself," they say. "What difference do my motivations make?"

This remark is not only snotty and off-putting; it's also dull.

I like writers who take the risk of explaining themselves. Through the years, some writers have ventured into the territory of accountability. Samuel Johnson said, "No man but a blockhead ever wrote except for money." George Eliot said, "It seems to me much better to read a man's own writing than to read what others say about him. . . ." And Evelyn Waugh said: "The last firm at which I solicited a job was engaged, among other things, in the manufacture of blacking. I pleaded desperately. If I wasn't employed there I should be driven to Literature. But the manager was relentless. It was no use my thinking of blacking. That was not for the likes of me. I had better make up my mind and settle down to the humble rut which fate had ordained for me. I must write a book. . . ."

Because I feel compelled to know why writers write, I also feel compelled to state my own motivations. It's sort of like a candidate's voluntary disclosure of personal wealth before an election: If I reveal myself, others will, I hope, be obliged to do the same.

I confess right now that I'd *like* to write for the money. When you make a lot of money as a writer, you get to meet Johnny Carson. (See page 124.) I've always wanted to meet Johnny Carson. But I don't want to be the guest who follows Bert Convy, Lola Falana, and the heart-attack doctor, although I'd like to meet Johnny before I'm eighty-three, before he's hooked up to a respirator instead of to Ed McMahon.

Write for money? Hell, I could make more money running a Xerox store, squeezing the blackheads of media doyennes (a job which seems to be reserved for émigrés from the Soviet bloc), or dancing at a Times Square sleaze palace with nothing on but a pair of Keds.

Of course there are alternatives. There are big bucks in writing advertising slogans, TV commercials, and self-help books. In fact, I could write a generational saga of lust, greed, and interracial dating and become almost as rich as David Rockefeller. (See page 177.)

But that's not what I write. I write satire. This has a curious effect on some people. What do you have against Joan Didion? they say. (See page 107.) What's wrong with "60 Minutes"? (See page 120.) Don't you like Ohio? (See page 143.)

What they are really asking is a twofold question: Why do I write funny? And, Why do I use humor to attack things? The answer to the first is elementary: As a little girl, my greatest pleasure was in making Dad laugh.

When Dad had had several martinis, we would talk. He told me he had always wanted to be a writer but decided to become a lawyer so he could make more money. This

was something that meant nothing to me, other than the
fact that I knew money was nice to have. After all, I lived
in a house with eight bathrooms, a spiral mahogany stair-
case, a marble hall with mirrors and a crystal chandelier,
and a fireplace in every bedroom, including mine. I knew
that not having money meant you were our gardener,
Peaches. Peaches was the nicest man in the world, but
why did he always drive around in those beat-up cars? If
being a writer meant that my father could not buy me
polo coats every winter, I was glad that he was a lawyer.

Still, I detected a certain amount of unhappiness in
Dad's career decision. During our martini chats, he always
got most excited about books. He told me about his favorite authors. He quoted poems and prose. He read aloud
from Edgar Allan Poe and recited Shakespearean verse.
Above all, he liked writers who made him laugh. In his
library he proudly displayed the complete works of S. J.
Perelman, Mark Twain, James Thurber. Around this time I
started to write parodies and send them to *Mad* magazine.
(I signed my name "Dean" instead of "Deanne" because
even then I noticed that writing funny was something
girls didn't do.)

I should explain that Dad always seemed to gravitate
toward anything marked "Ninety Proof." He taught me
how to mix martinis when I was six. I loved playing junior
bartender. It gave me a reason to participate in the world
of grownups. It made me feel important. It gave me something to do, other than wondering how to get an advance
on my allowance so I could buy more M&M's. By the age
of eight, I was an accomplished mixologist. I knew words
like *black olives* and *pimento*. (See page 85.) Fortunately
for me, Dad did not have a fondness for drinks that a
child would enjoy, such as Kahlua and milk. He had a
definitely adult taste when it came to drinking, and I still
consider martinis something that parents drink. I guess I
was lucky because I never wanted to be the kind of per-

son whose drinking habits were explained on joke cocktail napkins.

But as it is, I have enough problems. For instance, whenever I serve someone a drink, I expect them to recite "The Shooting of Dan McGrew." Moreover, I have been spotted on more than one occasion doing the Frug with Demon Rum. As a barroom sage once said, "Rum isn't drinking, it's survival." Whatever it is, my children will have a much simpler task than I did. They will be asked merely to pour and serve.

My first clue that there was more to life than mixing Dad's martinis came one day in third grade. I was sitting at the kitchen table doing my arithmetic homework. Our maid, Mattie, was cooking dinner. The phone rang. It was my best friend, Toby, who lived across the street. "Why didn't you tell me you were moving?" she said. I didn't know what she was talking about. "Don't you know there's a for-sale sign in your front yard?" I rushed out to look. There it was—a mysterious message had materialized in front of my favorite dogwood tree!

He had forgotten to tell me that we were moving, Dad said. I wasn't sure how to decode this report, but I knew that it made me mad. Several months later, after my parents were divorced, I received another news flash from Dad, delivered in what had obviously become his trademarked style.

It was a sunny afternoon in front of Silver's Temple. Silver's Temple was named after its patriarch, Rabbi Silver. The temple's real name was The Temple, but whenever anyone asked where you went to Sunday school, you just said Silver's. People were always impressed, maybe because Rabbi Silver once got to recite the opening incantation at the Republican Convention.

Sunday school had let out hours ago, and all the other kids had gone home. But I was still there, waiting for Dad. Silver's was the last white outpost in a once-elegant area of town that was rapidly becoming the kind of place they have to bus bus drivers into. The sight of a forlorn, pale child in front of a locked Hebrew temple in the middle of an urban Congo must have provoked comment among those straight enough to notice. I stood there for hours, wondering whether to turn myself in to the police, or cash in my HoJo Cola coupon at the Howard Johnson's across the street.

Finally a shiny red Corvette careened to a halt in front of the old sanctuary. It was Dad in his new car with the "Big Ed" license plates. He honked. As I ran toward him, I wondered why the Corvette was festooned with streamers. And why was the dashboard covered with flowers? "Oh, didn't you hear?" Dad said. "Joanne and I got married."

Joanne, you see, was the woman Big Ed was seeing after he and my Mom divorced. I resented the way Dad told me about his second marriage, but looking back on it, I take heart from the fact my family was not visited by other tragedies. What if my dog had been hit by a truck? I might have looked up in the sky and noticed an airplane skywriting the name "Rags."

Meanwhile, my parents had sold our thirty-five-room house. My mother, my sister, and I moved across town into a neighborhood, which for me was a trip to the Twilight Zone. Why did everybody's last name either end in a vowel or consist entirely of consonants? Who were these strange creatures who thought that wearing red and black on Thursday meant you wanted to get married? What planet was this, where the inhabitants ran around screaming that the Jews killed someone name Christ? "Christ who?" I kept asking, but everybody thought I was making a mean joke.

It didn't take long to find out who Christ was. Christ was the guy nailed up over every kitchen table in town. In perpetual agony, he—or He, if you will—oozed blood and

redemption as my friends gorged themselves on chicken
cacciatore, unless it was Friday, when the menu featured
deep-fried haddock with bottled fish sauce. For someone
whose dinners once consisted of filet mignon and cherries
jubilee, consumed under the watchful eye of a portrait by
Manet, this decor was disconcerting, to say the least. But
during those years, I spent a lot of time at my friends'
houses, eating whatever they ate. That was because Mom,
working at Thistledown race track as an exercise rider,
barely made enough to cover the rent, and Dad was always late with the child-support check.

I had to write all of this stuff down because I couldn't
believe it myself. Dad called to complain about having
trouble joining the all-WASP Oakdale country club, and I
was so broke I had to beat the tab for a Manner's Big Boy.
I started to write short stories about my neighborhood
and my way of looking at it. There was the teacher who
mispronounced *fictitious*. He said "fic-tee-tee-ous." Why
did I have to experience this ignoramus? Because of Dad,
that's why.

There was the guidance counselor who thought I had a
big future as an airline stewardess. Dad's fault, of course.
And who else made me endure a gym instructor whose
favorite expression was "Drop and give me twenty"? Mrs.
Todd ("The Bod") threatened to fail me in gym because
my gym suit was always wrinkled. According to a colorful
Ohio statute, if I had flunked gym, I wouldn't have been
allowed to graduate. To this day, I have recurring night-
mares about being stuck forever in twelfth grade because
I didn't iron my gym suit.

Yes— it was all Dad's fault! If he hadn't left my mother,
I would have been living comfortably in the section of
town where spectator pumps, seersucker suits, and creamed
chipped beef on toast were fashionable. Personally, I
never liked that stuff anyway, but I knew if you lived

near people who did, you didn't have to shoplift dinner.

If Dad hadn't left my mother, I would never have met people who thought that Wuthering Heights was a suburb of Cleveland! (See page 187.) Come to think of it, maybe we played them in football.

That's a joke I could never have told my girlfriends, because the only thing they ever read was *Peyton Place*. Over and over again (the hot part is on page 42). In fact, I kind of liked it myself. When I told my girlfriends I wanted to be a writer, they accused me of wanting to do something that only guys did. This was odd, because *Peyton Place* was written by Grace Metalious. Maybe they thought "Grace" was just something you said before dinner. The guys I knew didn't even believe that I really wanted to be a writer. When I told them I was going to college to study English, they accused me of "going after an M.R.S. degree." This was infuriating. I was at the point where I could easily have become the subject of headlines like "Teen Slays Parents, Self; Leaves No Explanation." Instead, I got busted for stealing a Temptations record from Zayre's Department Store.

Finally I caught the midnight express out of Cleveland. I headed for New York City, where I had enrolled at New York University. On my way out of town I stopped at Dad's office. "Are you sure you don't want to go to Cleveland State?" Cleveland State? What foresight! My Dartmouth-grad Dad wanted me to major in shop, so I'd have a skill to fall back on.

In New York, I felt as though I had emerged from the underground railroad. Today, whenever I walk past Rubin Hall, the student residence to which I escaped, I imagine a plaque that says: "At this site, depressed teens from Ohio got their first glimpse of freedom." And with my geographical liberation came the opportunity to learn a skill that has since been essential to my writing career:

asking for the check. By virtue of my parents' divorce agreement, Dad was to pay for my college education. Every semester, after I had spent hours waiting in line for my course schedule, they'd finally get to the S's, and then the bursar always said, "Sorry, Miss Stillman, we can't give you your course schedule. *Your tuition check hasn't arrived.*"

So every semester I dialed Dad. The check was in the mail. Several days passed. No word from Dad, but my classmates were having fun cutting class. I felt gypped. How could I cut class if I wasn't in class to begin with?

I dialed Dad again. His secretary had lost my new address, or so he said. I waited another forty-eight hours, and dialed again. Dad swore that he had mailed it off himself, but had somehow forgotten to put a stamp on the envelope. Maybe that's why I was later inexorably drawn to the world of magazines. Journalists spend a lot of time waiting for checks from middle-aged men who drink martinis.

Fortunately, college provided another outlet for my rage: By this time I was so pissed off that it didn't do any good to write—I wanted the whole world to hear my rage! I shouted it loud and clear from the barricades that sprang up around N.Y.U. I quickly realized that I wasn't the only one mad at my father. The whole country was mad at Dad, and everyone had a pretty good reason. The Dad in the White House was bombing Hanoi, the Dad in the university dean's office was ordering cops to tear-gas students, the Dad in the classroom was teaching Dad's warped version of history, and the Dad at home played golf with all of the other Dads. "The personal is political" went the slogan, and I switched my major from English to the more rewarding field of striking and chanting. (See page 158.)

I began to write for underground newspapers. These

makeshift journals were based on the idea that if you were
mad, you should let everyone know about it! Since college, out of which I dropped, I have continued this policy.
I think that shaking people up by making them laugh is a
hell of a lot more effective than phoning a radio talk show
to tell some windbag what you think, or penning self-
absorbed Op Ed think pieces.

Writing satire, to me, is a way to codify a topsy-turvy
world where R-O-L-A-I-D-S spells "relief" (see page 184),
where they produce life in the laboratory but can't manufacture a crumb-free English muffin, where women ask
men out for drinks and then worry about being too forward, and where a political party that espouses genocide
is considered sane because it condemns a would-be presidential assassin.

When I started to write for magazines (funny for
money, at last!), I began hearing from all of my relatives
—except Dad. He used to come to New York on business.
I'd know he was in town from the grapevine, but the guy
never phoned. Then my first book was published, a collection of humor by women entitled *Titters*. I guess it takes a
book with hard covers to impress some people, because I
got a telephone call. The voice identified itself as "your
father." Dad liked *Titters*, and said he had bought a dozen
copies and was telling his friends that his very own daughter had written a really good book. He said he always
knew I could do it.

I couldn't tell him then, or even during the few unsatis-
fying times we've spoken since, but his praise came too
late. My instinct to please Dad had made me a writer, but
my anger at him had made me a hard-core satirist, wielding wit like a zip gun, taking aim at the world, a perpetual
juvenile delinquent of letters.

That's why I write and write the way I do. I realize
now, however, that the original motivation has become a

small flame in a larger fire: Writing from now on will be its own reward. No longer will I be writing just to get back at Dad. And I'm through with being mad at him. Because, looking over this little essay, I think that I've just gotten even.

ADVICE

Stillman's Ten Most Unwanted List

For Assault with an Overused Article Idea

Mike Shapiro
    ALIAS: M. Shapiro
               Michael Shapiro
               Michael David Shapiro
               M. D. Shapiro
               Michael D. Shapiro
               Shap

    DESCRIPTION: Male, Caucasian, DOB 5/20/51, 5'10", 170 pounds, brown hair, brown eyes, records everything he hears with pocket-size cassette, currently at work on novel, screenplay, miniseries, and next month's column for *Argosy* magazine.

    VIOLATION: Shapiro was indicted by the Federal Originality Jury at New York City on March 12, 1976, for violation of Media Code 1341, Assault with an Overused Article Idea. Shapiro had reportedly contacted eighteen magazines simultaneously, offering a 3,000-word piece entitled "America's Shift to the Right." He was arrested on 6/8/76, and released after persuading an editor to post bond by

promising to write an article about his experience in court.
He failed to appear for arraignment on 6/15/76 and again
on 7/15/76. An arrest warrant charging possession of recycled article proposals and bond default was issued on
8/21/76. Shapiro has previously served time for penning
articles such as "Houseboat Life in Manhattan," "The
New Celibacy," "Should the CIA Be Abolished?" and
"Jill Clayburgh: The Woman Behind the Myth." Considered armed and extremely boring. If located, please keep
it to yourself.

For Theft of Personality

Frank Void

ALIAS: None

DESCRIPTION: Male, Caucasian, DOB 11/5/50, utterly
forgettable face, no distinguishing characteristics.

VIOLATION: Void was indicted by the Federal Felony
Bureau at Omaha on February 6, 1981, for violation of
Acceptable Behavior Code 876, Theft of Personality. For
the past six years, Void has attempted to entertain friends
and acquaintances with his impressions of various comedy
characters, appearing regularly at parties as Lily Tomlin's
Ernestine, Gilda Radner's Baba Wawa, Flip Wilson's Ger-
aldine, Steve Martin's wild and crazy guy, Laraine Newman's stewardess, John Belushi's Joe Cocker, and Danny
Aykroyd's Conehead. At an arraignment on 4/25/81, Void
pleaded no contest. He was sentenced to ten years of being himself, at which point he immediately fled the court-
room while calling out, "Excu-u-u-u-se me!" The judge
did not bother to issue a bench warrant. He has reportedly
been spotted several times since, most recently at his cousin's brother-in-law's finished basement, doing an imita-

tion of Rich Little imitating Jimmy Carter. If encountered, do not make eye contact.

For Transporting Sangría Across Interstate Lines

Marvin Jefferson
ALIAS: Mahrr-vinn
DESCRIPTION: Male, Black, DOB 8/12/45, 5'10", 185 pounds, planning to replace round bathtub with an octagonal one, ambition is to be Barry White.
VIOLATION: Jefferson was indicted by the Controlled Substances Board at Detroit on December 5, 1979, for violation of Contraband Code 789, Transporting Sangría Across Interstate Lines. The alleged sangría kingpin reportedly controlled the flow of the controlled substance along the eastern seaboard, and had been planning to "muscle in on the Midwest action," according to an FBI telephone wiretap. He was arrested on 3/18/80 while attempting to hijack a sangría-filled supertanker bound for Houston, and was released after offering the judge a wedge of Monterey Jack cheese. Jefferson failed to appear for arraignment on 5/7/80. An arrest warrant was issued. If invited to any sangría parties, please bring your own beverage.

For Telephone Fraud

Bruce McC. Cooper
ALIAS: B.C.
         Coop
         Mac

DESCRIPTION: Male, Caucasian, DOB 8/17/35, 6', 200 pounds, blond hair, hazel eyes, wears beeper, generally signs letters with "Cheers."

VIOLATION: Cooper was indicted by the Federal Telephone Squad at Chicago on September 19, 1977, for violation of Communication Code 2598, Fraudulent Use of the Telephone Wires. During a series of conversations with an undercover agent posing as a business associate, Cooper allegedly used the phrase "I'll get back to you" at least twelve times. He was subsequently arrested on 11/23/77, and released after posting a $10,000 nuisance bail. He failed to appear for an arraignment on 1/2/78, and was last seen dialing a colleague and saying, "Let's have lunch." Probably headed for the West Coast. If located, do not contact any member of any law enforcement agency, and immediately disconnect his telephone.

For Checkout Counter Holdup

Blanche Krupsak
    ALIAS: Mrs. Blanche Krupsak
            Mrs. Lloyd Krupsak
    DESCRIPTION: Female, Caucasian, DOB 4/3/39, 5'7", 155 pounds, brown hair, brown eyes, long-time ambition is to appear on "Family Feud" so she can kiss Richard Dawson on the lips.

VIOLATION: Krupsak was indicted by the Federal Works and Plays Well with Others Jury at Seattle on June 13, 1978, for violation of Behavior Code 92, Checkout Counter Holdup. Krupsak had allegedly appeared at grocery stores every Friday afternoon for ten years, at which point she purchased 150 dollars' worth of groceries, and then insisted on comparing the bill with the goods already

packed in grocery bags. Krupsak has been known to hold
up a line for hours with such queries as "What was forty-
nine cents?" "I thought the limes were eight for a dollar,"
and "Why am I being taxed for Chiclets?" She was released after posting a $15,000 bond, but failed to appear
for arraignment on 10/19/78. Since then she has reportedly held up hundreds of grocery store lines around the
country. If a witness to one of Krupsak's holdups, please
cause her to be sent to another city.

For Violation of the Celluloid Act

Vincent Carmine DeMarco
    ALIAS: Vincent
              Vin
              Carmine
              DeMarco
DESCRIPTION: Male, Caucasian, DOB 12/18/46, 5'5",
145 pounds, black hair, brown eyes, likes women who
have "a good chest," wears tailor-made socks.
    VIOLATION: DeMarco was indicted by the New York
State Film Board at Buffalo on April 14, 1979, for Violation of the Celluloid Act, a statutory offense which carries
a minimum ten-year sentence. DeMarco is known to have
made at least twelve movies about Italians who do nothing but hit their wives and say "Fuck you." All twelve of
these films have been widely hailed throughout the film
community as "searing." DeMarco was arrested on 7/2/79
after his latest film, *Dagos on the Rampage,* was nom-
inated for a Zabaglione, the highly respected Italo-
American Director's Award. He failed to appear for
arraignment on 10/5/79, and sent his cousin, Carmine
Vincent DeMarco, to explain why. DeMarco was last seen

in the executive suite of the Dow Chemical Studios, negotiating a deal for his next film, *Dagos on the Rampage,
Part II.*

For Refusing to Yield to a Higher I.Q.

Sue Crimmins
    ALIAS: Susan Crimmins
             Ms. Susan Crimmins
    DESCRIPTION: Female, Black, DOB 2/8/52, 5'6", 125
pounds, black hair, brown eyes, wears silk blouses that tie
at the collar, loves "being able to communicate with the
public."
    VIOLATION: Crimmins was indicted by the Federal
Grand Jury at Washington, D.C., on August 11, 1979, for
violation of Subchapter A of the Intelligence Act, Refus-
ing to Yield to a Higher I.Q. Crimmins had been on the
television network's tragedy beat for six years, and had
not once asked an appropriate question. She was arrested
on 10/15/79 after filing a report about a sniper attack in
which she asked one of the wounded victims, "Why do
you think this happened?" Crimmins was released after
signing a declaration of sensitivity, but failed to appear
for arraignment on 12/18/79. Although her microphone
had been revoked upon her original arrest, she has since
buttonholed as many as twenty-two eyewitnesses to violent crimes, and asked such questions as "What was the
assailant really like?" "Tomorrow was Angie's birthday,
wasn't it?" and "Do you think the death penalty is a deterrent?" If approached at a crime scene by Sue Crimmins, please cause the perpetrator to ask an intelligent
question.

For Felonious Decision Making

Jane Marie Callahan
 ALIAS: Jane
 Jane Marie
 Stupid
 DESCRIPTION: Female, Caucasian, DOB 3/10/48, 5'5",
120 pounds, hums Ferrante and Teicher tunes in the
shower, puts A.1. Sauce on everything, currently at work
on trimming her cuticles.
 VIOLATION: Callahan was indicted by the National
Board of Inquiry on August 10, 1981 for violation of Citi-
zen Code 923, Felonious Decision Making. The fifty-
fourth American hostage in Iran, Callahan refused to leave
Teheran along with the other captives, despite an intensive international campaign to bring about her release,
including an offer to do a guest-spot on "Love Boat."
When asked by an Algerian diplomat why she chose to
remain in the Middle East, Callahan cited "superior
souvlaki" and the amount of money she now saves on
Nair. She is currently under indictment in both the United
States and Iran, and is undergoing trial in the latter country for removing her chador and attempting to have it
dry-cleaned.

For First-Degree Harassment

Bob Francis
 ALIAS: Robert Francis
 DESCRIPTION: Male, Caucasian, DOB 10/22/52, 5'8",
145 pounds, has no favorite colors, thinks *Animal House*
was sophomoric, currently writing songs about rejection.
 VIOLATION: Francis was indicted on November 15,

1980, by the Federal Communications Jury at Boston for violation of Conversation Code 562, First-Degree Harassment. During a six-month period, Francis reportedly engaged dozens of coeds at cocktail parties around town in discussions of such topics as the intellectual decline of America, the childishness of sports, and Ann Beattie's use of italics. Francis was arrested on 1/15/81 and released after subjecting cellmates to an analysis of foreign filmmakers. On 3/15/81 he was arrested again, for staging an impromptu street performance of Hamlet's soliloquy. Francis failed to appear on 4/2/81 for arraignment, and was last spotted at the Whitney Museum's Dali Retrospective. Approach at your own risk.

For Gross Negligence

Barry Stein

ALIAS: Stein

DESCRIPTION: Male, Caucasian, DOB 9/18/51, 5'10", 185 pounds, brown hair, hazel eyes, got "clean for Gene" McCarthy in 1968, voted for Ronald Reagan in 1980 because McCarthy endorsed him.

VIOLATION: Stein was indicted by National Value Board at Chicago on December 2, 1980, for violation of Job Code 845, Gross Negligence. Stein rose rapidly through the junior executive hierarchy at Allied-Schmitz Petroleum Industries, and until recently was Vice President in Charge of Public Relations. He was arrested on 1/16/81 after holding a press conference in which he announced that oil spills have actually been known to aid the growth of plankton, and thus are an integral element of the human food chain. Most reporters refused to reprint his statement, except for the one from *Fortune,* who was subsequently indicted as a second-party defendant. Stein was released after posting $20,000 bond, but failed to appear for arraignment on 2/8/81. It is rumored that he will soon resurface in two capacities: as consultant to the Environmental Protection Agency, and as public relations chief for Industries Without a Face, a new brokerage house specializing in toxic-waste futures.

The Etiquette of Getting High

Oh my God—roaches in the punch bowl—hash oil on the sofa—burning joints on the coffee table! What's a hostess to do? And what about those much more damaging, personalized breaches of all that is sacred and well bred: those coarse refusals of proffered weed, just because it's Mexican—vulgar ingratitude that would fully justify social ostracism or, in the Muslim countries, hideous lingering death. And what is one to do about those churls who blow their coke the wrong way—or those unsavory boors who inhale more than their fair share? Though informality is the rule in high society, certain types of behavior simply *will not do*.

Manners aren't everything, of course. The proper hip host or hostess knows, for example, how to steer the conversation away from those unorthodox, boring, and incomprehensible discussions of politics, religion, and stagflation. After all, there is no substitute for *joie de vivre!* But a little attention to the amenities of high life never goes unrewarded: Just follow the few simple tips herein, and you'll be able to give—and have—a high time with style, elegance, and grace.

Let us begin by considering the seemingly simple matter of pot politeness. Marijuana, of course, may be smoked in all sorts of ways. Surely every group of pot smokers has its own rituals concerning the consumption of pot. However, there is a right and a wrong way to use marijuana. Make sure, for example, that your smoking stash is efficiently cleaned before smoking: A joint that suddenly erupts in a person's face with a loud (and sometimes embarrassing) seed-pop is truly revolting. Maintain the cleanliness of your water pipe by checking the bowl every ten to fourteen days for stagnant water, algae, barnacles, sludge, and other fetid material. (Heavy tokers are advised to fumigate their bowls weekly.) It's a good bet that nobody enjoys having his or her throat seared by a nice, long toke on a joint rolled with inexpensive paper. Perhaps you may want to stock up on some higher grades of rolling paper—or else maintain a handy supply of throat lozenges. Moreover, sloppy joint rolling will not guarantee your popularity with others, particularly the eagerly toking guest whose lap has just been littered with a torrent of seeds, stems, and buds.

Proper placement of accouterments is essential. Ashtrays, for example, should be convenient to each guest, thus avoiding the inconvenience of makeshift roach receptacles. Guests should avoid using wastebaskets, unlighted fires, empty fireplaces, potted plants, or any dishes that have been used for food as an ashtray. (Dropping a roach into your host's toilet—and then not flushing it—is definitely bad manners.) There are some guests, of course, who regard themselves as human ashtrays, swallowing any and all roaches that pass their way. The wise host or hostess will take care to please the roach-eating guest by passing marijuana butts to this person.

While smoking the joint, one should make an effort not to drool or slobber all over it. Nobody enjoys being passed a joint that has been drenched in someone else's saliva or phlegm. Should you be the recipient of such a joint, it's advisable not to hold it aloft and shout, "Who's the asshole who upchucked all over this joint?" Chances are, no one will answer, and you'll be left trying to pass a joint that nobody wants to touch.

Since your guests' feeling of well-being always comes first, no one should ever be urged to smoke pot once he or she has refused. Neither should any guest feel uncomfortable because he or she would like some more. If a person says no to grass, perhaps the host should offer a soft drink, wine, or beer. Maintain the ambience of the drug, though; it is not desirable to offer a nontoking guest a hit of crystal methedrine, for example, while the other guests are so stoned they are having difficulty lifting a joint to their lips. Those who are not smoking will undoubtedly get a contact high simply by being in the smoke-filled room. (And household pets will generally be rendered mellow if they are reclining in the smoking area. Hence it is not necessary—or civilized—to blow marijuana smoke into an animal's face and thereby cause it to become comatose.)

Cocaine is enjoying a vogue these days; consequently it has become very expensive and there is a highly complex ritual surrounding its use. The wise cocaine consumer will want to protect his investment by thoroughly familiarizing himself with the etiquette of this delightful white powder. Don't be surprised, for example, if your guests refuse your coke because they have watched in horror as you divided your snowy mountain into lines by using a dirty razor blade. A line of coke laced with hair stubble and flakes of dried shaving cream is undoubtedly unacceptable.

On the other hand, if your guests are snorting your coke, the considerate host will not want to impose upon them by repeatedly asking, "Isn't this the best coke you've ever tasted? Well, isn't it?" Wait for your guests to smile and perhaps run amok as they tell you what they think. (Dealers, of course, may solicit opinions, since they are in the business of discussing the quality of their wares.) As a host you will want to make snorting easy and comfortable for your guests. Therefore, such paraphernalia as empty ballpoint pen tubes, cardboard Tampax dispensers, and worn-out one-dollar bills is only to be used during snorting emergencies.

If a guest accidentally leaves a trace of snot on the snorter, you should discreetly substitute a clean snorter. (The considerate guest may avoid the possibility of depositing a nasal calling card on the coke spoon or snorter by making sure to blow his nose before indulging.) Further embarrassment can be avoided if cocaine is tasted with the index finger, as opposed to use of the little finger, which may cause others to assume you are picking your nose.

Perhaps a guest has mistakenly blown out through the snorter instead of snorting in, and 500 dollars' worth of cocaine now lies fanned out across the carpet. Obviously the guest possessing the pair of misdirected nostrils will be terribly chagrined, and this unfortunate situation must be handled delicately. Calling the guest a cab, for instance, will not recover the precious crystals of cocaine, nor will it endear you to the other guests who, although they may be dismayed over the loss of their potential buzz, are as capable as the next person of committing a similar faux pas. The most practical course, it seems, is to turn the party into an orgy and ask those interested to remove their clothing and place themselves on those sections of the floor where the cocaine has been blown. Your investment will not be totally irretrievable, as guests will be able to absorb the coke through their skin, and most everyone will enjoy the added surprise of coked-up sex. The guest who caused the orgy, though, should not be invited to your next party.

Upon occasion, you may find yourself as a guest at someone else's party where cocaine is not being offered, although many of the guests are sporting golden spoons around their necks, evidently anxious for a taste, should it appear. You have brought along a small supply and desire to share it with two other friends. Naturally, you will have to snort outside the main party area. As you and your two friends head for a private snorting area (usually the bathroom), try not to make your intentions overly obvious, otherwise you may be trailed by a stampede of eager guests afflicted with an uncontrollable case of "Hoover nose." Perhaps your trio should slip away one at a time and meet in an unusual place, such as the garage, thereby enabling the three of you to snort in peace as everybody else flocks to the bathroom. On the other hand, you may wish to remain in the main party area and offer everybody a little sample. Simply remember that whatever you decide will make a lasting impression upon the other guests, and the wisest course of action may serve to establish you as a Metternich of cocaine diplomacy.

Another high that is quite popular these days is nitrous oxide, often referred to as laughing gas. The protocol of laughing gas differs greatly from that concerning most other drugs because there are only a couple of ways of introducing NO_2 into your system, neither of which requires expensive paraphernalia. When throwing a nitrous party, all the host need have on hand is a full tank of gas and a large supply of balloons. An adequate balloon supply is of prime importance since the balloons often break or pop while being pumped full of gas, or become waterlogged with unsightly globules of spit (as gas is often sucked from the same balloons repeatedly).

A big annoyance to the nitrous host (and everyone else) is the problem tanker. While social tankers casually inhale a balloon or two at a time, the problem tanker is known to go right on sucking far into the night and may even collapse several times, usually on top of the tank so that no one else can reach the nozzle. How far should a host or hostess go in an effort to control this uncomfortable situation? The best course, it seems, is to treat the problem tanker just as you would any other guest. Bring him a large balloon filled with laughing gas every so often, as you would your other visitors. Try to keep the tank as far away as possible, as it will be too tiresome for him to get up and stumble toward it. If you are stuck with an incorrigible tanker who, no matter what you do, cannot pry his lips from the tank nozzle, gently remind him that inhaling nitrous oxide in that manner is dangerous. Point out that as a "tank hog," he is in bad form. As a last resort, politely ask him not to "Lloyd the tank."* Of course, it is wise to omit this individual from all subsequent guest lists, but if for business or family reasons his presence cannot be avoided, simply keep a sharp eye on the source of supply, keep track of each round, and lock up the tank after you're finished. Should the tank hog become violent despite repeated hints and suggestions, it is advised that he be courteously eighty-sixed.

The well-mannered consumer of laughing gas will also want to impress upon his or her dentist a thorough knowledge of nitrous decorum. Don't, for example, sign up for root-canal work fifty times per year just so you can tank up in the dentist's office. It is not advisable to enter your periodontist's office and shout, "Hey, Doc! Turn on the gas!" Nor will you be a welcome patient if you are caught placing the inhaler over your nose and turning the gas up full blast when the dentist is on the telephone. It pays to remember that the discreet social tanker is welcome anywhere, especially the office of a sympathetic dentist who knows that dispensing a little bit of the chuckle wind can't hurt his practice.

* As in Lloyd Bridges, start of "Seahunt"; equivalent of "Don't [Humphrey] Bogart that joint."

The protocol of pill popping is often ignored, with dis-
astrous results. Perhaps the most common gaffe occurs
when unidentified pills are passed around at a social
gathering and guests neglect to ask what they are, for fear
of somehow appearing unsophisticated. Actually this atti-
tude is quite naive, and may lead to unpleasant consequences such as nausea, unexpected acid trips, allergic
reactions, or worse. If you do not know whether you're
being offered a soporific, barbiturate, hallucino-tab, or hay
fever pill, it is better that you ask first, rather than become
ill later and blame it on the host. Should you swallow a
tab of acid, wittingly or not, and soon after decide that
you'd like to "fly," refrain from doing so. Jumping out a
window while tripping is definitely bad manners, and the
thoughtful guest will not want to bring heat down on the
host.

If you see a mound of pills on your host's dining room
table and instantly recognize it as your kind of buzz, do
not grab a handful and scarf them up. Wait until you are
offered (and unless you are partying at the pad of a pill
pincher, you will certainly be invited to sample every
delicacy on the menu).

Sometimes the partying may grow a bit tiresome, and
you're able to consume only half a pill. Try not to make
the pill crumble into a jumble of tiny grains while cutting
it in half, as this can cause others to beat you to a bloody
pulp. Such a silly predicament can be avoided by halving
the pill carefully. Neither the edge of a dime nor your car
key will do in this case, and as for your two front teeth,
never mind—unless you possess a pair of fangs. If wor-
ried about your paring abilities, it may be wise to ask a
more experienced person to halve the pill for you.

If you are the kind of person who enjoys Quaaludes, be
careful with your host's valuable possessions. Although
you may fancy yourself a graceful individual while 'luded
out, your muscles are actually relaxed beyond the point of

normal control. Hence it is suggested that you keep your clumsy mitts off the stereo. Moreover, if enjoying carnal pleasure in this pleasant state, try to remain as alert as possible. An excited partner isn't likely to appreciate the humor of snoring during a heated session of *soixante-neuf*, nor will the dozing recipient of a blow job be a likely candidate for a repeat performance.

On the other hand, if you prefer speed, try not to bore your partner with endless heavy rapping. You will know this uncomfortable situation has occurred when your partner reaches into her handbag and dons a pair of ear plugs.

Certainly there are ground rules concerning the use of other drugs, such as glue, cough syrup, and dry-cleaning fluid, but it isn't necessary to discuss them at this time. Manners, to be sure, improve the quality of any high and ensure one's popularity with others. To paraphrase Ralph Waldo Emerson: "I could better get high with one who did not respect the truth or the laws than with a sloven and unpresentable person. Moral qualities rule the world, but at short distances the senses are despotic."

Ann Van Brothers Talks to Teens About Your Hair, Your Figure, Your Diet, Your Sweat, and Your Face

With special thanks to the American Girdle and Brassiere Council, The American Council for a Germ-Free America, The American Depilatory and Deodorant Council, and The American Frozen Pizza Lobby.

Start with the Basics

Like I always say, there's no time like the present to start with the basics. So let's start with the basics. The most essential element of grooming, aside from not emitting unpleasant smells (see chapter on filth), is neatness. Nothing tees me off more than the sight of a potentially pretty young lady dressed in a well-coordinated outfit without the proper foundations underneath. What I am referring to, future adults, is flab on the loose. There is absolutely no reason for unsightly fatty deposits to remain unchecked, when they can easily be controlled with one or two simple undergarments.

If, for instance, your thighs resemble piano legs, then perhaps you should consider purchasing a girdle. It may be difficult at first to put it on, so don't hesitate to thoroughly grease up with something that really works, like 30-weight Quaker State Motor Oil—and hop in! However, there is the remote possibility that you may resemble a human cannoli after donning the girdle. If so, you have obviously purchased the wrong undergarment. Nowadays, trusses are available in designer colors. Don't hesitate to buy several.

When it comes to brassieres, proper fit is the most important consideration. Personally, I myself am rather boyish-looking up top, if you read me. I have tried just about all there is to increase the size of my bustline. Right now, in fact, I am practicing the power of positive thinking. As I write this sentence I am thinking big, firm, and *luscious*. In the meantime, I am perfectly willing to entertain any suggestions you might have (no pectoral exercises, please; they didn't work in junior high, and they won't work now), so please send them to Ann Van Brothers, c/o Joyce Van Landers, Opinionated Columnist Newspaper Syndicate, Deadline, Ohio.

Still, I make the most of my figure by actually wearing an entire *false bust*. Don't laugh! My fella hasn't yet gotten the message, and we've been dating for eight years. Because I'm such a good girl, we've never gotten past fooling around *down there* (see chapter on filth), and whenever he wants to touch me above the waist, I simply refuse. That's all there is to it.

As for you full-figured girls, well, my condolences. By full-sized I do not mean B or even C cup. I'm talking D, E, and triple F here, girls. The only thing you can possibly wear under your clothes to contain all that cleavage is, let's face facts, a cargo sling—and even then, think of how long it takes to iron those things! (Let's not underestimate the importance of wrinkle-free brassieres.) I honestly feel

sorry for you full-figured girls, and the best I can do is
offer this heartfelt tip: Think of your bust as your thighs
(which, if they're as big as your knockers . . . well, I
think you get my drift), and your brassiere as just another girdle—and you'll be a walking lingerie department.

Let's Talk About Your Face

To quote myself, "Your body is like a four-speed,
twenty-watt hair dryer. When it's on, sometimes it doesn't
work, and when it's off, sometimes you forgot to plug it
in." In other words, put your best foot forward, because if
you don't, you might trip and hurt yourself. What this
means is that if your hairdo is not right for the shape of
your face, you could be in big trouble. Let's examine the
classic facial shapes and see what coiffure goes with
which type.

R H O M B U S

WRONG   RIGHT

A common facial type, the rhombus allows for a wide variety of
coifs, with the exception, of course, of the inappropriate "Barbara
Walters" style pictured on the left. Note how the correct hairdo
highlights the classic rhomboid cheekbones.

TRAPEZOID

WRONG   RIGHT

The trapezoid is unusual, to say the least, and should therefore be treasured like a rare jewel. Unfortunately, it looks pretty weird, and I'm afraid there's not much you can do about it, other than insure your face and hope nothing causes it to turn into an . . .

OCTAGON

WRONG   RIGHT

Well, it could be worse—you could have easily been a dodecagon instead. So thank your lucky stars that there are only eight corners to your face rather than twelve. The most effective way of concealing the corners is wearing the versatile "grocery bag" shag.

PARALLELOGRAM

WRONG   RIGHT

Now enjoying a vogue, this shape can be tricky. If hair is kept scrupulously in place, the parallelogram is—are you ready for this?— unparalleled in the looks department.

RIGHT TRIANGLE

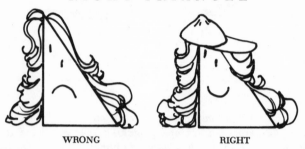

WRONG   RIGHT

Oh-oh! This highly improbable facial structure plagues only a tiny fraction of our teen population. Generally the right triangle–type is not seen at junior-senior powwows, school picnics, and drive-ins. The style on the right should eliminate this devastating problem. However, as for that other problem endemic to this particular facial shape—the uneven placement of the eyes—you're on your own, kid. Good luck!

You Look Like Your Food

Just between you, me, and the lamppost, girls, I know that your daily diet generally consists of a lot of carbos, topped off by a couple swigs of Romilar. Personally, I have nothing against this diet—particularly the cough syrup. In fact, the only thing wrong with it is that it can cause your face to assume the qualities of a topographical roadmap, as my steady once pointed out to me. And was I ever grateful to him! He said that my face made him barf, and that's just the word he used, too—barf! I simply had no idea that my diet was causing my face to erupt in clusters of tiny white pustules just aching to be squeezed and popped! I was convinced that, like most of our other problems, my disgusting complexion had something to do with being a woman, and I had resigned myself to a lifetime of bad skin. "It figures," I remember thinking as I pondered the difficulties of being female. But fortunately for me, I had my boyfriend, who works for the frozen pizza lobby, to tell me that all I had to do was stop stuffing my face with Mallomars all day long, and switch to something healthy and nutritional, like frozen pizza.

Naturally, I watch my complexion in other ways, too. Since I am a busy career woman, I cannot afford the luxury of a facial, which can take up to sixty minutes of my precious time. Generally, I kill two birds with one stone by steaming open my clogged pores as I stand over a hot stove cooking dinner! Last week, for instance, as I slow-cooked chili con carne for a dinner party of twelve, I simultaneously steamed my face—and now I look like a million bucks. Of course, I can't quite seem to stop smelling of jalapeño peppers (see chapter on filth), but who ever said that beauty would be a breeze? Beauty is *not* a breeze, and I don't care who says different.

What About Hair?

Remember Iran? Well, when it comes to bodily hair, I basically have one thing to say—FEH! Get rid of the stuff, pronto! Since you'll be spending a good portion of your time bathing (see chapter on filth), hair removal should be a simple task. And unsightly hair growth should never be allowed to get out of hand. It's not only repellent to the opposite sex, but it accumulates unpleasant odors (see chapter on you-know-what). So, girls, keep those legs and underarms smooth, and a special note to those young ladies with—oh, I can't even say this, I'm going to have it put in mirror writing—riah melborp on your face—take it from me, you look pretty funny. Either stay inside, fuzz-face, or do something about your looks!

A Few Words on Filth

One of my favorite sayings is "If you don't clean your own house, you'll have to pay someone else to do it. Usually they don't even show up, and if they do, they'll probably overcharge." I like this saying because I said it. Translated into teen jargon, it means you're only as pretty as you feel—or *eel-fay*, if you read me. Naturally, in order to eel-fay etty-pray, you have to ell-smay etty-pray. And in order to smell pretty, you've got to bathe regularly. This does not simply mean you must take a bath or shower once a day. Girls, I'm talking two, three, maybe even four showers every day. That's right. Every day. Why? Because germs are everywhere, and a young lady in the fast, modern, push-button world of today can get pretty filthy, if you get my drift.

For instance, did you ever put a red nylon blouse in the wash with the whites and then put the whole thing on the spin cycle when it should have been (a) separated, and (b) on gentle wash? Sometimes, that's the way life is, and when that happens all you can do is take a shower, because you're probably upset as it is, and you know what upset means. Upset means nervous perspiration, if you can imagine that. Unfortunately, I can, and it makes me barf. Speaking of barf, make sure to bathe immediately after tossing your cookies, even if you are still not feeling well. As soon as those icky smells are washed away, you'll feel almost as good as new.

Now, supposing it's morning and you've just awakened. Your body is coated with perspiration from the previous night's sleep. Yes, even if you've slept calmly, your pores often work overtime busily secreting disgusting fluids all through the night. These foul fluids must be washed away as soon as you wake up, lest you spend the remainder of the day offending your friends as you accumulate even more smells. Which is not hard to do.

For instance, consider walking to school, to the store, to a friend's house, or even across your bedroom to the telephone. This simple exertion causes certain muscles to flex, thus sending a message to various glands, which in turn causes you to, well, *sweat*. Frankly, sweat is filth and should be washed away quick as a bunny. If you find yourself sweating in the presence of others and unable to wash immediately, perhaps you should simply excuse yourself and leave. But get to a shower a.s.a.p. These smells can linger for days!

Somehow, this brings me to the perilous world of dating. It's important to bathe at least twice before going out on a date, just to *make sure*. Before stepping out with my beau, I make sure to spray myself with plenty of Lemon Pledge, not only because it smells so refreshing, but also because it forms an impenetrable layer of protection which can last for days! It also prevents any of his smells from rubbing off on me, and we all know how easily that can happen. Of course, after a date, I make sure to bathe in a superhot tub and a capful of Pine-Sol (a quart if I've gone to third base).

I am sure that many of you already suspect that there is one time of the month during which you can't take enough hygienic precautions. I'm talking menstruation here, girls. You know—the time when a friend is visiting, or the roof just happened to fall in. This is a particularly dirty, not to mention trying, time of month. My advice is to simply take the entire week off and consider it the privilege of being female. That's what I've been doing all these years. As a matter of fact, I'm in bed at this very moment, jotting down my advice to you. Sometimes I even sneak in a few extra days off by sequestering myself in my dressing room during ovulation, another unpleasant bodily phase.

But no matter what your body is doing, the rule is: Treat your body like a sink full of dirty dishes, because it can easily become one. That's what my mother used to tell me, and boy, am I ever grateful. Excuse me, I've got to shower. I'm just covered with ink! Besides, I'm waiting for my boyfriend to call. He always calls when I'm indisposed. So I think I'll just hop in the shower, sing a few bars from my favorite song, "Let It Be Him," and I'm sure my pink princess phone will ring its little heart out.

LITERATURE

THE STORY OF

Withdrawals and Deposits

SOON TO BE A MAJOR MINISERIES . . .

ALREADY A BEST-SELLING NOVEL . . .

PRESUMABLY A WAY OF LIFE

The Barbara Hoffman Agency
80631 Madison Avenue
New York, NY 10023
(212) 995-4888
3/10/80

Dear Jonathan:

Really enjoyed our lunch the other day at Akasaka. Here's the manuscript I told you about. It's a remarkable new women's novel called *Withdrawals and Deposits*, written by a courageous new writer whom I am proud to represent, Marilyn Literary-Guild. I'm certain that this book is going to make a big splash, and that we'll all be hearing a lot from Marilyn in the future.

Enclosed is the introduction and an outline of the first sixteen chapters. As I mentioned to you at lunch the other day, I feel that you are the perfect editor for this book. Your sensitivity to the conflicts of the contemporary women is well known. Furthermore, you are regarded as an editor who is unafraid to explore new literary territory. This is why you are the first editor to be accorded the privilege of reading *Withdrawals and Deposits*. I'm certain that you will enjoy Marilyn's work as much as I do, and I'm looking forward to touching base with you soon. Thanks,

Barbara

P.S. Just to remind you—the deadline for bids on *The Charo Book of Health and Beauty* is one week from today.

The Barbara Hoffman Agency
80631 Madison Avenue
New York, NY 10023
(212) 995-4888
3/10/80

Dear Lindsay:
Really enjoyed our lunch the other day at Vesuvius. Here's the manuscript I told you about. It's a remarkable new women's novel called *Withdrawals and Deposits*, written by a courageous new writer whom I am proud to represent, Marilyn Literary-Guild. I'm certain that this book is going to make a big splash, and that we'll all be hearing a lot from Marilyn in the future.

Enclosed is the introduction and an outline of the first sixteen chapters. As I mentioned to you at lunch the other day, I feel that you are the perfect editor for this book. Because you are a woman, you are sensitive to the conflicts which we are all experiencing. Furthermore, you are regarded as an editor who is unafraid to explore new literary territory. This is why you are the first editor accorded the privilege of reading *Withdrawals and Deposits*. I'm certain that you will enjoy Marilyn's work as much as I do, and I'm looking forward to touching base with you soon. Thanks,

Barbara

P.S.   Just to remind you—the deadline for bids on *The Charo Book of Health and Beauty* is one week from today.

WITHDRAWALS AND DEPOSITS

by Marilyn Literary-Guild

A modern women's novel in which
everything hangs in the balance . . .

Introduction

The main problem was that they all wanted something. They wanted things that I couldn't give them. But I never said no. I tried to give them whatever they wanted. Of course, I wanted things too. I never got them. I think that was because I was so busy giving that I didn't have time to receive. Now I have audited my books and decided that my life is in arrears. My relationships are morally bankrupt, my expectations are severely inflated, my thoughts are operating at a dangerous deficit. The accounting procedure left me in a state of deep depression, yet when I finished, I felt like I had received a check for $1,000 because the bank made a mistake in my favor. . . .

June 1980
My agent's summer house
Cape Cod, Massachusetts

Chapter 1   *Phil*

Phil was my husband. There was only one side dish he ever ate with dinner. It was Birdseye beans and spaetzle, but only the spaetzle. I decided it was time to cash in my chips and become a novelist.

Chapter 2   *Jane Eyre*

Jane Eyre was my collie. She wanted her stomach scratched whenever I watched old movies. So did I, but no one was there to do it. I scratched Jane Eyre's stomach, and got nothing in return.

Chapter 3   *Pam*

Pam was my aerobic dance teacher. She wanted me to know what aerobic meant but I did not think that was necessary. She wanted me to breathe like this—pant, pant, pant, exhale; repeat—but I never really did that either.

Chapter 4   *Christopher*

Christopher was the fetus I aborted. I knew the fetus was male because I had dreams. Had I had Christopher, I know he would have wanted something from me that I could not possibly have given—but would have tried.

Chapter 5   *Mother*

Mother was my mother. She wanted me to stop taking my silk blouses to the dry cleaner and wash and iron them myself. It was a good idea, but why are mothers like slot machines that never stop giving you quarters?

Chapter 6   *Rob*

Rob was my lover. We did everything together, including flossing. But I picked up my floss and threw it out. He didn't. Chalk up another emotional overdraft.

Chapter 7   *Jamey*

Jamey was my six-year-old daughter. She wanted me to do her homework. But what about my homework? Life was homework, and there was never anyone to give you a dollar for getting an A.

Chapter 8   *Willie*

Willie was my acupressurist. He wanted to know why I had so much tension in my shoulders. It was another case of a man wanting something I couldn't deliver.

Chapter 9   *Butch*

Butch was the parking lot attendant. He wanted a blow job. I gave him one, once. I have yet to see any dividends. Now I am playing hard to get.

Chapter 10   *Norma*

Norma was my best friend. She wanted the name of my haircutter, the person who hangs my wallpaper, and a good travel agent. I Xeroxed my Rolodex and gave it to her. She still owes me the favor. But she really doesn't have any good contacts.

Chapter 11   *Mauro*

Mauro was my greengrocer. A real piece of ass. He wanted me to size up his arrugula. I did and felt used, like someone had stolen my checkbook, forged my name, gone to Madrid, and had a good time—as me.

Chapter 12   *Dr. Moore*

Dr. Moore was my gynecologist. He wanted to know whether I used a diaphragm or the pill. He didn't know because he couldn't find my chart. Bank makes mistake in their favor. Do not pass Go.

Chapter 13   *Jimmy*

Jimmy was my first lover. It was in tenth grade. He said it wouldn't hurt. It did. He said I wouldn't get pregnant. I did. He said he'd marry me. He tried to, but I wouldn't let him. The ledger was temporarily balanced.

Chapter 14   *Father O'Chaste*

Father O'Chaste was my priest. I once confessed to him about everything I had ever done that was bad. He wanted me to confess for everyone who had ever done bad things to me. I did. It didn't matter. He didn't see that I was confessing for him too. For a while I thought this was enriching. But it wasn't.

Chapter 15   *Rabbi Silvergold*

Rabbi Silvergold was my rabbi. He wanted me to be happy. I converted to Judaism not to be happy, but so that I could suffer more and I could have something really worth feeling guilty about. Then I started feeling guiltier than the other members of the congregation, which, although rewarding in the short run, offered little of lasting value.

Chapter 16   *Baba Doug*

Baba Doug was my meditation counselor. He wanted
me to meditate so that I could focus on what I was doing
at a particular time. It didn't work because all I could think
about was Baba Doug without his clothes on. I had in-
vested too much time, and the odds on the payoff were a
hundred to one.

Note: Chapters 17–58 to come.

> Jonathan Talbot
> Respectable Books
> 12267 Third Avenue
> New York, NY 10031
> (212) BU 8-9543
> 4/15/80

Dear Barbara:

Thanks for giving me the chance to read *Withdrawals
and Deposits*. I wish I had received it a week earlier, because I just signed up a similar book called *Creative
Bookkeeping*, a women's novel by an exciting new voice
on the fiction horizon, Laura Subsidiary-Wright. Thanks
just the same for letting me take a look at Marilyn's work,
and I'm looking forward to lunch next Thursday. Best,

P.S.   I'm afraid I'll have to pass on *The Charo Book of
Health and Beauty*. The consensus here is that it's a good
idea, but not a great one. Regrets.

Lindsay Gross
Prestigious Publishing House
150226 Avenue of the Americas
New York, NY 10049
(212) CH 3-4567
4/20/80

Dear Barbara:

Thanks for giving me the chance to read *Withdrawals and Deposits.* I think it has a lot of potential (West Coast: po), but I'm not sure the author can carry it off. In order to drum up support around here, do you think I could see a sample chapter? Otherwise, I'm afraid I can't quite picture the whole ball of wax. There may also be a slight problem with the sales people, but if I can get behind Marilyn 100%, I think sales will be a piece of cake. Anxious to hear from you,

Lindsay

P.S.   Sorry, but I'm going to have to pass on *Charo.* The consensus here is that it's a great idea, but the distribution people think that due to Charo's controversial nature, they won't be able to crack the southern market.

The Barbara Hoffman Agency
80631 Madison Avenue
New York, NY 10023
(212) 995-4888
4/27/80

Dear Lindsay:

When I first mentioned your request to Marilyn, she was understandably upset. She said that she couldn't possibly write a sample chapter because she won't know how each chapter will read until she actually sits down to write the book. I said I knew how she felt, but that you had expressed high regard for her work and therefore it would probably be a good idea for her to put a little more effort into her presentation. I am happy to report that Marilyn agreed to write a sample chapter, which I have enclosed. I think it's quite a bold piece of writing, and I'm sure you'll agree. Hope to talk to you soon.

Barbara

Sample Chapter   *Ardith*

Ardith was my therapist. She wanted whatever I wanted. I wanted to know why my life was a ponzi scheme in which every relationship threatened to collapse the pyramid. Ardith asked me if I thought I knew the answer to that question. I said I would think about it. Then she asked me if writing a book about all of this would make me feel better. I'm still waiting for the psychological check to clear, and when it does, I'll know what the balance is. But until then, I'm living on uncollected funds.

Lindsay Gross
Prestigious Publishing House
150226 Avenue of the Americas
New York, NY 10049
(212) CH 3-4567
5/15/80

Dear Barbara:

As per our conversation on the phone yesterday, herewith the contracts for *The Maugham Years*. Frank is anxious to begin research and has already booked a flight for London.

Also, there is a lot of enthusiasm on the seventh floor

for *Withdrawals*. In fact, Sy has authorized me to discuss a six-figure offer, so let's work something out at lunch tomorrow, okay? How about Mr. Chow's?

Lindsay

P.S.   I *love* Ardith. She sounds real. Is she? I'm just asking because we may have to clear the characters with Legal.

THE NEW YORK TIMES BOOK REVIEW,
March 18, 1981

A Mirror for the Eighties

WITHDRAWALS AND DEPOSITS
By Marilyn Literary-Guild.
New York: Prestigious Publishing House.
$12.95.

By Leonard St. John

It's difficult to be objective about a book that has received so much advance publicity. We have all heard about the enormous advance garnered by Mrs. Literary-Guild for *Withdrawals and Deposits*. And certainly we are all wondering about the forthcoming "major miniseries," which has reportedly compressed this volume that weighs as much as a small child into 23 hour-long episodes to be aired over a one-month period. All of this is generally considered bad news for the writer of less commercial fiction.

Be that as it may (and I'm not so sure that it should), it must be pointed out that the author has penned a work of major import. Several of my colleagues, in fact, have even ventured so far into vocabulary land as to label Mrs.

Literary-Guild a "white Toni Morrison." Now, about this I must comment. Although meant to be complimentary, this equation comes across as somewhat arch. Even worse, it does not really give credit where credit is due (which is not to take anything away from Miss Morrison's rightfully attained status—though I'm wondering: Of whom is she a black version?). The authority with which Mrs. Literary-Guild speaks catapults her into a lofty circle of penpals (look, Ma, I'm writing!). One thinks of Jane Austen, Mary McCarthy, Doris Lessing, Elizabeth Hardwick, Eudora Welty, even Billie Holiday at her most succinct and earthy. In years to come, *Withdrawals and Deposits* can only be viewed as a new frontier, a Pike's Peak, a Continental Divide which the author, in her daring literary odyssey, has courageously crossed. Her use of language is dazzling, her insight formidable, and (I know this may annoy my live-in friend, but I'm going to say it anyway) her looks are a disconcerting turn-on. In fact, if the Jill Krementz snap on the dust jacket is any indication, and it usually is, the author can only be described as an American Liv Ullmann.

Don't be put off by the hyperbole of flacks and ad men. Mine is better because it's written by a book critic. To say it simply, this book towers over all fiction by women published during the last two years. It totally engages the reader, it's a disturbingly honest story, one that should not be missed because it's a refreshingly candid virtuoso exercise, an astonishing first novel that dares you to pick it up and then, when you do, you're grateful for this antidote to acid rain, reruns of "Laverne and Shirley," Brooke

(*continued on page 30*)

How to Become
a Rock Critic in Seven
Easy Lessons

1. *Isolating the Primary Facts*

Just as college journalism students learn the comprehensive "Five-W" lead (who, what, when, where, why), the rock journalist must learn the multifaceted "Two-W, One-H" lead, which swiftly dispenses with at least one of the following crucial queries: Where were you when you received the record album?* What were you doing when you received it? How many times have you listened to it? Here are some examples you would do well to emulate:

> I first heard "Heart of Gold" when my friend Bill Berkson (whose neighbor Tom Clark wrote the picture/poem *Neil Young*) played me the *Live at Anaheim* bootleg, just after Ellen's baby was born, the day I left Bolinas.
>
> PAUL WILLIAMS
Soho Weekly News

* Since the successful rock critic often reviews the same band a number of times, the question "Where were you when you heard the group for the first time?" may be substituted.

. . . I very nearly enjoyed my 30th through 138th hearings of this album's [*Kung Fu Fighting*] title track. . . ."

JOHN MENDELSOHN
Rolling Stone

When I received [*Luther's Blues* by Luther Allison], I was entering my house. When I saw the record, I grabbed it and hurried over to a friend of mine's apartment, to listen to it on their superior (to mine) sound system.

JOEL DILLER
SunRise

. . . One night last summer I was lying in bed watching rock and roll on television. It was about two in the morning and I was trying to lull myself to sleep. On came the new Eric Burdon Band and I sat bolt upright. Eric was hot. . . .

STEPHEN DAVIS
Rolling Stone

I loved her [Lorraine Ellison] previous album in 1969, and I liked this for a while in 1974, but the more I listen the more I noticed how much she shrieks, and when I play the previous album, it sounds more limited than I had remembered.

ROBERT CHRISTGAU
Creem

I bought an Al Green album about two years ago, Call Me. I just heard he was good, and there was nothing else I wanted to buy at the time. I didn't play it very much. I don't think I played it at all.

GEORGIA CHRISTGAU
Creem

2. *Creating a Vivid Scenario*

Occasionally the setting of your story will overshadow the rock star about whom you are writing. When this occurs, you will most likely be on assignment in the state of California, covering an important rock concert, interviewing a rock personality on tour, or assessing a onetime rock star's attempt to make a comeback. As you write your re-

view, remember that an exact and vivid word picture of
the magnificent California geography will draw immedi-
ate reader response. For example:

> The searing California sun turned a brighter orange as it set
> slowly behind the mountainous moustache of David Crosby.
>
> ROBERT SMITH
> *Crawdaddy*

> The Los Angeles sun shone brightly outside, and a storm cleared
> the air so thoroughly that Pete [Townshend] was astonished to
> see the city's surrounding mountains for the first time. . . .
>
> BRUNO STEIN
> *Creem*

> A diamond mist sticks to my windshield as irrepressible night
> cat Tom Waits and I take off on a deserted Santa Monica Boule-
> vard in my '69 Chevy.
>
> RICH WISEMAN
> *Rolling Stone*

> The rustic house on Round Valley Drive in the hills of the San
> Fernando Valley is in one of those pockets of geography that
> provides a uniquely California retreat for those who can afford
> one. . . .
>
> TOM NOLAN
> *Rolling Stone*

> On a recent trip to California (highlights of which included: at-
> tending a taping of the new Dinah Shore show, with special
> guest James Franciscus; driving 50 miles to Disneyland only to
> find upon arrival that Disneyland is closed on Tuesdays during
> the winter; seeing Joe Don Baker in the flesh at an all night
> restaurant; putting my hand in Wally Cox's pawprints at the
> snack stop during the Universal Studios tour; watching a solid
> week of Fractured Flickers reruns), I had the good sense to . . .
>
> BILLY ALTWAY
> *Creem*

L.A. is a great big freeway they say, pay a hundred down and
buy a car, if you don't you won't get very far. Tooling down
gaudy Sunset Boulevard on a typical smog-smeared Los Angeles afternoon, the cab driver is busily pointing out the sights

to the first-time visitor whose New York cool is being steadily chipped away by the lethargic fantasy-world that calls itself a city.

VERNON GIBBS
Crawdaddy

3. The Function of Voice

Readers of rock criticism like to know exactly who is reviewing their favorite musician. As a rock critic, you will have ample opportunity to let the reader know you. For example, during your career you will often find yourself inside the very hotel room of a particular rock personality. If mentioned in or near the beginning of the review, this interlude will subtly establish your credentials by implying that you may have actually watched Alice Cooper apply his mascara, snorted the cocaine of Iggy Pop, or shared a bottle of Ripple with a famous blind blues singer. Here are some of the better "Hotel Room" leads:

Shifting his wooden leg on the Holiday Inn bed and reaching for his fifth of whiskey, Furry Lewis eyed the cans of beer in the plastic wastebasket that had been packed with ice and pressed into service as a cooler.

WALTER DAWSON
Rolling Stone

Lonnie Jordan is drunk and fucked up, weaving around the lobby of the St. Regis Hotel in Detroit, approximating the agility of a bull in heat.

Crawdaddy

Just another Holiday Inn Friday night in Harlingen, Texas. Downstairs in the El Cid Lounge, Dapper Bobby Denisio chinks his way through "Honey" on jaundiced Steinway keys as travel-numbed citrus buyers and Margarita-giddied steno queens evanesce in the dim.

NICK TOSCHES
Creem

We are sitting in a wind-whirled cold out here, poolside at the
Holiday Inn in Belmont, a suburban town five minutes away
from the Circle Star Theatre where [Al] Green is performing.

BEN FONG-TORRES
Rolling Stone

Later, slumped in a hotel room, the decidedly un-foppish Brit-
isher [Robin Trower] marvels over his newly acquired popularity.

ED NAHA
Creem

His [Gamble Rogers'] life, as glimpsed in the stale shadows and
rumpled sheets of a rented room, seems almost a cipher, a cruel
caricature of the 20th-century American troubadour. You look
around and see a battered guitar case, an old suede jacket, a
toothbrush with the bristles chewed down, and you can't help
wondering what makes a 37-year-old lonesome picker named
Gamble Rogers go on.

PAUL HENDRICKSON
Rolling Stone

4. *Variety Through Colloquialism*

Rock criticism that displays a sense of history is always
popular. Many reviewers make sure to color their criticism
with stylistic references to the early days of rock culture,
flavoring their prose with a dramatic mixture of street
slang and New Journalism. Originated by critic R. Meltzer,
this type of review bears a particular hippie-to-hippie
tone that is important in preventing outsiders from understanding it. Here, for example, is R. Meltzer demonstrat-
ing "Meltzer Prose" for *The Village Voice* in a review
titled "Doodoo Plus Weewee Equals Haha":

In the spring '67 early ancient primordial days of the rock crit
bandwagon as critters up at Crawdad Magazine always knew
there was still one place to go after freebie feelers for any stuff
in town had been summarily nipped in the bud: just take our

asses over to the Cafe au Go-Go for the Mothers' nitely whatsit
and they always let us in without much complaint even tho we
never reviewed em even a paragraph worth.

Other fine illustrations of "Meltzer Prose" include:

Okay, boys and girls—a lot of facts this time around . . . And
they're going to be coming at you fast, so sit up, pay attention,
and ferchrissake try to look interested.

Ian MacDonald
Creem

The Tough Will Inherit The Whole Tube. [John] Kay believes it
for *sure*. Is some bad bizniz he's meanin in that tune what all
with these clockwork wild boy-animals huntin down the Bur-
roughs anarchic cataclimax. And this [Steppenwolf] ain't no
bloose band either. . . .

Bruce Malamut
Crawdaddy

TIME FOR SOME PUD PULLING! What else can you do at
10 in the morning? So if you're lucky there's a press release somewhere in with all the records, an 8½ x 11 piece of paper for
you to whiz off on. You can always jack off onto the sheets but
that way you can't save on the stains. Whereas with paper you
can. In a month you can have a collection of twenty-five-plus
cum-stained bios and itineraries in all the pastel colors of the
rainbow including grey. So it sure must have been a shocker for
all those reviewers to receive their Arthur Miller album without
one shred of excess matter in the package: nothing but a record!

R. Meltzer
Fusion

5. *Emphasis Through Repetition*

Often, an important point can be made most effectively
by repeating certain key verbs and adjectives. In rock
criticism, the culinary lexicon is a never-ending source of
inspiration, enabling you to repeatedly stress the oral na-

ture of rock and roll. Do not submit a review for publication without at least one conjugation of the infinitive "to cook," or several variations thereof (synonyms such as "to brew," "to sizzle," or "to smoke"). Types of food should be mentioned for added emphasis, particularly if you possess a singular knowledge of soul food. The following examples demonstrate skillful use of the culinary lexicon.

Hotter Than Hell cooks from start to finish with the boys in the band sounding tighter and more lethal than in the past.

> ED NAHA
> *Rolling Stone*

Listen to the way they [Eric Burdon] cook on "Don't Let Me Be Misunderstood."

> BARRY TAYLOR
> *Crawdaddy*

Rod Stewart may have been at his essential best . . . with that high pressure cooking band, The Faces. . . .

> JAN HODENFIELD
> *New York Post*

The urgent, unsettling strings that bring on the end . . . are usefully tart marinade for a genteel reading of Paul Anka's "You Won't Matter Any More."

> FRED SCHRUERS
> *Crawdaddy*

A heavy metal primer, the recording [Led Zeppelin] dishes up a dollop of sexuality.

> HENRY EDWARDS
> *New York Times*

After working the low tones into a mean, thick brew, he [Todd Rundgren] whipped it on the crowds.

> GORDON FLETCHER
> *Circus Raves*

It took Steve Barri, ABC's resident AM hitmaker, to forge Kinky's [Friedman] crude bizarre worldview into a commercially palatable brew. . . .

> LARRY SLOMAN
> *Crawdaddy*

. . . Clifton [Chenier] is rice, liver, and pig blood stuffed in hot
intestines and served with cheap red wine. Pure funk.

DAVE HELLAND
Crawdaddy

. . . Jack Bruce and Felix Pappalardi cooked up Cream while
Eric [Clapton] still had BB's [King], Freddy's [King] and Albert's [King] chitlins in his back pocket.

Crawdaddy

6. *Style with Punch*

Many rock groups engage in such onstage activities as
the smashing of guitars and amplifiers, and mock murders
and mutilations. Hence, it is often difficult to avoid the
subject of violence in a rock review. While piecing together your critical composition, you will undoubtedly discover that the musical emphasis on destruction has forced
you to bend and twist your language to describe it. Be
inventive and follow your impulses. Bear in mind that specially created hyphenated adjectives and military hyperbole add sparkle and punch to coverage of rock violence.

With twin guitars hammering out catchy mondo-distorto riffs
and bass and drums amiably bringing up the rear, Kiss spews
forth a deceptively controlled type of thunderous hysteria closely
akin to the sound once popularized by the German panzer tank
division.

ED NAHA
Rolling Stone

. . . King Crimson were full-blast electro-attack.

BRUCE MALAMUT
Crawdaddy

Going through the violence riff for shick effect only, he [Marc
Bolan] was careful not to let the macho-destructo routine get
out of hand.

STEVE WEITZMAN
Zoo World

Concocting a terribly English sound teeming with cocky vocals, nastier-than-thou guitar playing and almost too-lush-for-words arrangements, the group [Kiss] presents itself as being a hybrid of classic Yes, Queen, and middle-period Bowie.

ED NAHA
Swank

If you like meta-volume, para-intellectual rock, you will like [Blue Oyster Cult]. . . . The group, as butch and black leather as any band averaging 5'7" can be, proved that Zep punk-prole aggression . . . has been replaced with bleak amphetamine rage. . . .

DAVE HICKEY
Zoo World

When the Funkers [Grand Funk Railroad] are riding on that hot and heavy locomotive on stage it's like being in the middle of a musical nuclear explosion. . . . Donnie Brewer starts slugging out his distinctive pulsating beat. . . . Sandwiching guitar and skins with a heavy dose of . . . bass and [Craig] Frost's nimble fingers on the keyboard, they [Grand Funk Railroad] amplify the mix loud enough to deafen laboratory test rats and produce the Grand Funk sound that's loved by fans around the globe."

STEVE GAINES
Circus Raves

He [John Kay] was A-1 Nazi but not tuff.

ROBOT A. HULL
Creem

7. *Building a Vocabulary*

The creative rock critic will want to pepper his or her reviews with words and phrases that demonstrate thorough knowledge of the rock world. Let the reader know, for example, if the subject of your review has "paid a lot of dues." Let the reader know if the music in question has "classical roots." (It is not necessary to name the source of the roots.) Mentioning the make of a guitar, as in "Fender Stratocaster" or "Chet Atkins Gretsch," lends resonance to any review. Refer at least once to the rock group as an "aggregate." If stumped for the appropriate word or phrase, the following rock and roll vocabulary should be helpful:

axeman (guitar player)

cerebrofunk (a nitty-gritty outpouring of soul with a mystical flavor)

chops (ability to play)

funk (a nitty-gritty outpouring of soul)

funky (full of funk)

gritty (funky)

intelligent raunch (any funky sound you would like to elevate)

lungsman (singer)

Muscle Shoals, Ala. (site of an important recording studio hallowed for its army of accomplished studio musicians)

rimshot (drumming on the side of the drums)

roadies (men who go on the road with rock groups to care for and carry their equipment and set it up on stage)

session cats (those who accompany the person or group during the recording session)

Southern fried funk (funk from below the Mason-Dixon line)

spacy, yet earthy (an otherwise indescribable sound)

subtle brilliance (for devoted fans only)

viscerally pleasing (you can dance to it)

zen funk (a nitty-gritty outpouring of soul with an Eastern flavor)

The Art of
Menu Language

Menu language is a colorful folk art and merits placement alongside such literary Americana as the tall tale, yellow journalism, confession magazines, and comic books. Indeed, the American menu is undoubtedly more influential than the daily press: it can be surmised that the number of people who have been persuaded by a newspaper editorial to vote against a school bond issue instead of for it hardly equals the number of people who have been persuaded by a menu to order "smothered chicken" instead of "ind. can tuna."

Yet the intellect which conceived such wonderfully evocative and widely used terms as "bed of lettuce," "boat of lettuce," and "nest of lettuce" has never been properly acknowledged. It is time to rectify this situation, as we re-examine our roots in this third century of America and salute the innovative thinking which has shaped our nation.

For example, consider carefully the following list:

1. surf and turf
2. rib and reef
3. beef and reef
4. ship and shore
5. land and sea
6. hocks and scales

Obviously, all are synonyms for the phrase "fish and meat"—or, to be crude, "fish and flesh."[1] Yet, to this researcher's knowledge, the actual phrase "fish and meat" appears on nary a menu. Nor does the even simpler distillation "F and M." Why? One can only assume that American ingenuity has reached its height here, never yielding to the urge to simplify and always searching for new and better ways to offer a product. (Item number 6 on the above list is an invention of this writer's. Yet is not that invention itself great tribute to the channel of thought menu language has only begun to explore?)

Now, let us consider a phenomenon in which various combinations of fruits or vegetables are described *melodiously*. An excellent example of this mode of menu language is the phrase "fantasia of fruit." Derivatives are "medley of fruit," "rhapsody of fruit," "symphony of fruit," and . . . well, the mind reels with other possibilities.[2] At a time when Americans seem to have grown stale in other creative endeavors, it is heartening to discover such imaginative use of language.

After the musical food metaphor, we must examine that wonderful series of descriptions which have only a hyphen in common: "lightly-dusted," "piping-hot," "farm-fresh," "country-fresh," "garden-fresh," "fresh-caught," "fresh-caught in the morning surf," "corn-fed," and "milk-fed."

1. "Fish and flesh" is a copyrighted phrase, in anticipation of future use as the name of a restaurant.
2. After years of study, this researcher has not discovered the term "carrot duet" or "rutabaga concerto." Would anyone with such examples of menu language please submit them in care of the publisher?

And there are those all-purpose nouns "festival" and "riot" which frequently succeed the kind of food which is served in the plural: spaghetti, clams, oysters, or mussels.

Have you ever seen an oyster riot?[3] When your veal arrives, do you know if it is corn-fed or milk-fed? Is there a difference between piping-hot and too hot? Does it matter whether or not your scallops were "harvested in the morning from the cool, deep Atlantic"? Certainly these questions are but a nuisance to the dedicated menu scribe, who stirs his words with a large measure of poetic license and not a pinch of consumerist caution.

Any inquiry into the art of menu language cannot overlook spelling. In this intriguing aspect, American menus are a salute to our abiding spirit of independence. For example, while the phrase "dressing à la maison" may be spelled correctly on one menu, chances are it will appear as "dressing la maison" or "dressing masson" or even the cunning "house dressing a la masson" on others. "Salad Nicoise" enjoys a rich variety of incarnations, as does "Veal Cordon Bleu" (or "Blue," "Blu," or "Bleue." Take your pick). With the recent popularity of Middle Eastern food, a fascinating array of new misspellings now appears on American menus. The word which is spelled the most different ways is "falafel." Is it "felafel"? Or "felefel"? Or "felafell"? Or is it "souvlaki"? Alas, these questions may never be answered.

Finally one must consider the infinite variety of appellations attached to that all-American favorite, the hamburger. There is the Big Mac, the Big Chef, the Big Chock, the Big Budd, the Big Boy. There is the Pop Burger, Mom Burger, Teen Burger, Jr. Burger, HoJo Burger, California Burger, and Little Boy. Certainly it is a fluke of one menu writer's mind that "Big Boy" and "Little Boy" are also the names of the World War II bombs dropped on Hiroshima and Nagasaki. Or is it?

3. Or an oyster melee?

And so, as Americans stagger dyspeptically into their third century, the question "Whither menu language?" takes on new meaning. History has shown that it is an eclectic form. It is able to bend with the times, as when a delicatessen sandwich fondly known as a "Marv's Special" suddenly becomes a "Barry's Treat" under new restaurant ownership. It is independent of the strictures of grammar, as in the rendering of the noun "fountain" as an adjective, to wit: "fountain delight." Furthermore, it makes lots of people hungry. And what could be more enduring than that?

The Feminish Dictionary: A Guide to Defining Ourselves

FORMERLY DEANNE STILLMAN

While women are busy trying to rewrite history and to write and create our own herstory, the language we speak still largely reflects today's male-dominated culture whose hirsute antecedents made up this one-sided lexicon way back when they could get away with it. Except for the minor concessions of bodies of conferences, assemblies, and too few influential newspapers to the use of such now-proper qualifiers as *spokeswoman* or *chairperson* instead of the archaic *spokesman* or *chairman,* there has been virtually no mass acknowledgment of our language's gender problems. There has been no comprehensive reform within new editions of dictionaries. And worst of all, there has been no reform even among the speakers ourselves.

As attempts to define anything must make use of the

language and speech that we already know, then the definitions themselves often assume an inadvertent bias. If we as women are to define ourselves meaningfully, then the language itself must be able to accommodate these new definitions; otherwise, the attempt is undermined at the very beginning. In order to facilitate such sorely needed self-definition, I propose a new women's language, based, of course, on the vocabulary which we already use, but always reflecting *in every aspect* the female object of a particular reference. This new language will be called *Feminish*. In it all references to men will be deleted and replaced with references to either women or all sexes in general when necessary, unless the object of a certain remark is a *self-defined* male, like Frank Sinatra. (If gender is unknown, the unisex rule shall apply.) This means that all syllables like he, male, males, man, men, son, and other more obscure though equally sexist usages of exclusively male references will be wiped entirely from the English language.

We begin at the most obvious point. The very word that man long ago decided to call his counterpart was *woman*. Why *woman*? Because it was merely an extension of the word *man*! We have no moniker that is truly our own! Therefore we must take the next logical step on the road to real self-definition, delete the second syllable *man* and insert temporarily the allegedly nonsexist and currently preferred label *person*, so that *woman* becomes *woperson* (pronounced wo' person). The word *person*, however, has for its second syllable the exclusively male noun *son*, and is therefore unsuitable, so *son* must be replaced by the truly nondiscriminatory noun *one*, so that *person* becomes *perone* (pronounced per own'). Thus *woman* becomes *woperone* (pronounced wo' per own). This new label will be hard to get used to, but after several months' usage, I am quite comfortable with it, and even my friends are beginning to address me correctly. When alone, I practice: I am a woperone, you are a woperone, she is a woperone, and we "women" are all wo . . . people. (*Women,* with the second syllable *men,* is unacceptable.) This change also applies to such nouns as spokesperson, doorperson, seamsperson, layperson, journeyperson, yeoperson, ombudsperson, etc., and even the word female must be altered to the more fair and meaningful term *feperone,* which rhymes with *pepperone,* the sausage that goes on pizza. The transformation of the plural, *females,* would naturally be *fepeople.*

These changes, however, although most basic, are just the beginning. We mustn't forget that *every single noun* applying exclusively to males should and will accommodate the hitherto unacknowledged existence of fepeople, and, more urgently, we must pay attention to our own speech so that corrections begin to come automatically. While comprehensively studying the language, I have discovered that wopeople are inadvertently discriminated against in thousands and thousands of words. To list each and every offender and its new incarnation would consume an entire lifetime, but once you understand the rules, creation of Feminish is as easy as finding your clitoris. Following are just a few examples of our new vocabulary, with a possible manner of usage included with each. As with all languages, there are exceptions to the rule, and they, too, appear herein.

The Feminish Dictionary:
A Guide to Defining Ourselves

Amanda = Aperoneda
Her name is Aperoneda and
she comes from Alabama.

amen = apeople
Apeople!

**bedfellows = bedsisters,
bedbuddies**
Politics makes strange
bedsisters.

cockatoo = cuntatoo
Feperone cockatoos are
cuntatoos.

cockney = cuntney
Cuntneys talk funny.

cockpit = cuntpit, genitalpit
The stewardess and the pilot
are getting it on in the
genitalpit.

**cocksmanship =
cuntswoperoneship**
That's cuntswoperoneship!

**cocktail = cunttail,
genitaltail**
I'll have a genitaltail, please,
straight up.

Adam's Apple = Eve's Apple
She should have that Eve's
Apple taken care of.

**Frosty the Snowman =
Frosty the Snowperone**
(little girls need to identify)
Frosty the Snowperone was
a very funny creature.

Fu Manchu = Fu Peronechu
(in case of female offspring)
Don't mess with Fu
Peronechu.

Girl Friday = One Friday
Wanted: Versatile and
Groovy One Friday!

German = Gerperone
The Gerperone people are a
clean people.

hemorrhoids = shemorrhoids
Many lady bus drivers are
afflicted with shemorrhoids.

human = huperone
(pronounced hup'er own)
The huperone race is near
extinction.

hymen = hything
She popped her hything
while riding a bike.

**"I, a Woman" = "I, a
Woperone"**
Have you seen *I, a
Woperone*?

Isle of Man = Isle of Perone
Several years ago there was a rock festival on the Isle of Perone.

Katmandu = Katperonedu
Many hippies live in Katperonedu.

Landlord, landlady = landperone
Hey, Phyllis, should I answer the door? It's the landperone!

manage = peroneage
My hair is hard to peroneage.

Managua = Peroneagua
Peroneagua, Nicaragua

mañana = peroñeana
The Spanish people never do anything until peroñeana.

Henry Mancini = Henry Peronecini (for his daughter's sake)
Henry Peronecini used to be named Henry Mancini.

mandate = peronedate
The people's peronedate.

mandrake = peronedrake
In certain cultures perone-drake root is a cure for lumbago.

Manhattan = Peronehattan
I'll take Peronehattan.

Man-o'-War = Perone-o'-War
(gender not obvious)
Perone-o'-War won the Kentucky Derby.

manipulate = peroneipulate
You're just trying to peroneipulate me.

maniac = woperoneiac
Was Lizzie Borden a woperoneiac?

midwives = midhusbands, midspouses
The opposite of midwives is midhusbands.

Alfred E. Newman = Alfred E. Newperone
What, me worry?

menstruation = wopeoplestruation
Wopeoplestruation is a feperone bodily function.

omen = opeople
A full moon is not a good opeople.

shuttlecock = shuttlecunt, shuttlegenital (depends on who's playing) Badminton is played with a shuttle-genital.

Rumania = Ruperoneia
The national bird of Ruperoneia is the fly.

Do You Type in the Nude?

For what reason is higher value placed on the poetry of Robert Frost or T. S. Eliot than the verse of, say, Buddy Hackett? Or Dyan Cannon? These are difficult questions that literary critics—those self-appointed arbiters of taste —will never dignify with answers. And yet, celebrity poetry is a rich source of inspiration for many Americans. Muhammad Ali's rhymes are quoted by kids in the street. The poetry of Leonard Nimoy, Richard Harris and Richard Thomas appears on many household bookshelves alongside the works of Rod McKuen and Judith Viorst. On the "Tonight Show," recitations of verse by Red Buttons and Jack Palance move listeners to tears.

Ah, the show biz bard! Will his work ever be read in college classrooms? Is he content to be acclaimed for one talent and not the other? Such queries might cause even the most determined *écrivain* to divest himself of thesaurus, typewriter and other creative accouterments. But not so the celebrity rhymester, who has no fear of literary obscurity and happily continues to wax poetic in public.

Indeed, celebrity poetry is a pure and inspirational form, the very existence of which raises many provocative questions. For example, how do celebrities with extremely busy schedules find time to write poetry? Who are their literary influences? How do they explain the preponderance of religious metaphors in their poems? Do they type in the nude?

Our literary inquiry is best begun with Buddy Hackett, whose frequent television and nightclub recitations of verse make him the "Poet Laureate of Hollywood." Hackett's career as a poet began several years ago when he recited a modest rhyme on the "Tonight Show." Johnny Carson remarked that it was lovely. The audience responded enthusiastically. And the editors at the Nash Publishing Corporation on Sunset Boulevard—who happened to have tuned in to "Tonight" that night—scrambled to sign up this budding bard. Soon, Nash published Hackett's first collection of poems, *The Naked Mind of Buddy Hackett*.

On the book jacket is a photograph of a naked Hackett —with a strategically placed top hat—reclining impishly on a psychiatrist's couch. He is being scrutinized by a note-taking, fully dressed Hackett seated in a chair. In the background is an illustration of a goat, underneath which is printed the name "Joe." A dead duck hangs upside down from a coat rack. Hackett designed the cover and calls it a metaphor for his life. "The guy on the couch is completely exposed to his shrink," he explained in a phone interview from the Sahara Hotel in Las Vegas, "and the shrink is confused. The dead duck is the patient looking for help and the goat in the background is my pal Joe from Chicago. He's the kind of guy who's always there when you need him."

Symbolism plays an important part in the Hackett *oeuvre,* as in such poem titles as "A Message From My Electric Lights" (i.e. from his brain) and "Big G" (a reference to God), and the line "My sheets are blank/I've naught to give." Imagery, too, is a device favored by the chubby comedian. For example, the poem "My Mother" begins with the couplet "Your love made the gold look dull today,/Your eyes made the cold feel warm today"—

an obvious allusion to the sparkle and warmth of the senior Mrs. Hackett. Similarly, "Genesis in Durham, NC" (site of the Duke University diet clinic) contains the line "The scale is my god of smile or frown," in which the lower case "g" in the scale-god equation signifies Hackett's belief that the scale he weighs himself on is an important scale, even a god-like scale, but should not be confused with the real God, who is more important, and the subject of several other poems.

The structure of Hackett's poetry is classic, often employing the alternating rhyme pattern technically referred to as the AB scheme. This frequent use of the AB couplet may be significant: when Hackett began his career as a comedian, one of his most popular routines was an imitation of a Chinese waiter who continually repeated, "One from Column A, one from Column B, not one from Column A and B." The meter of Hackett's poetry, like the clipped pattern of his speech, however, is casually imprecise, as in the couplets

> *Blue is my world*
> *sans clouds or storms*
> *Around me is sunlight that dries and warms*

Although his poetry is reminiscent of the early and more structured work of Rod McKuen, Hackett insists he has been influenced by no one. "I don't read any other poets," he says. "If people read a poet, it's because they need it. My poetry is me." And it comes out just about everywhere, he says. "Sometimes I'll be walkin' along and I get a brainstorm. Other times I'm drivin' with my wife and a poem comes to me and I say, 'Sherry, take this down.' I write my best things on doilies in restaurants when I'm waitin' for a sandwich."

H₂O MY GOD

The black water is a teasing lover
It does not keep you,
It swirls and whirls and dances to entice you—
It lies calmly waiting, showing
the cool warmth of comfort,
Naively you volunteer your love
And your flesh;
Your love is taken and destroyed
At once—
And, at its leisure, the black, thieving, lying water
Regurgitates your body.

BUDDY HACKETT

TIME FLIES *(excerpt)*

Time flies
it flies timelessly
into a page of nothingness

Strangers touch
with touching hands
touchingly
a deep meeting
fleeting time
disentangles
gentleness
pushing fingers into memory
nothing will remain
only
the warm planted wild-flowers of impression
a glow in winter
a love song sung in the palm
reflections of a distant future
mirrored in today's yesterday
time

washes
nothing is removed
it only dries the fingertip tears
that smears
the ripe departure . . . .

RICHARD HARRIS

From *I, In the Membership of My Days*
by Richard Harris. Copyright © 1973 by
Limbridge Music, Ltd. Reprinted by
permission of Random House, Inc.

UNTITLED

days
when hands are empty
and
fingers reach out from moving doors
and pained windows
unreciprocated
where
the frost in the heart
thaws
in the old age of memory's house

LEONARD NIMOY

Reprinted from *Will I Think of You?*
by Leonard Nimoy. Copyright ©
1974. Published by permission of
Celestial Arts, Millbrae, California.

LIBERATION DAY *(excerpt)*

. . . . *Well Hallelujah and 'ole hot damn.—I'm*
cookin in love's frying pan—delicious
delectable easy to chew and ready to
share a bite with you—cause if I love you
like I love me, then our problems are
over with don't you see? So do whatever
you have to do—always holding that in
your point of view and our great big

> *world will finally be what it's always*
> *been that we couldn't see.*
> 　*And we Are free.*
> 　*Cause that's the way it's intended to be.*
> 　*Golly!!!*

DYAN CANNON

Printed with permission of the author.

Does Buddy Hackett type in the nude? "No," he says, "I write 'em out in longhand."

A recent entry into the ranks of Hollywood rhymesters is Dyan Cannon. Her poetic aspirations were made known to the world when she recited an introspective meditation titled "No One Can Take the Pain Away" on "The Merv Griffin Show." "I wrote it while in a down period," she explained via telephone from her Malibu home. "It was difficult to recite. But I think everyone's been through what I've been through and people should talk about it."

Not long ago, Cannon recited "Liberation Day" (printed in part here) on the "Tonight Show." She had been inspired to write it, she said, by the plight of Rubin "Hurricane" Carter, incarcerated until recently in a New Jersey penitentiary for a triple murder many believe he did not commit. "I've known some men who carry prisons around in their heads," she says, "but even though Rubin's behind bars, he's one of the freest men I've known." Interestingly, "Liberation Day" was penned on one of Cannon's "topless days." "I feel freer," she says, "wearing just a bikini bottom and no top."

In the tradition of the most poignant revolutionary poetry, "Liberation Day" puts forth a highly political message. For example, the lines ". . . as I sit here and don't/know how to pay the rent, or the laundry/man, or the big tough lawyers with their get-even plan" are particularly significant because they examine the inequities of a capitalistic society. Loosely adhering to the form of blank verse, the poem employs a rhyme scheme that is unique for both its grass-roots simplicity ("delicious/delectable easy to chew and ready to/share a bit with you") and its folksy use of pejoratives to complete a rhyme, as in the final couplet, which rhymes the infinitive "to be" with "Golly!!!" Cannon also demonstrates broad knowledge of poetic technique in her deft use of the phrase "Hardy harr harr," a classic example of onomatopoeia.

Perhaps the most prolific celebrity poet is Leonard Nimoy, the pointy-eared and cold-hearted Mr. Spock of "Star Trek." His poetry collections, *You and I* (described on its cover as "a fresh and powerful love story") and *Will I Think Of You?* ("a passionate narrative poem by the internationally known star"), were published by Celestial Arts, a small house in San Francisco. Both books were republished recently by Dell and Avon due to the "Star Trek" fans' constant clamor for Nimoy memorabilia.

Nimoy prefers free verse to other poetic styles, writing most comfortably in the stream-of-consciousness mode, unhampered by the strictures of rhyme, meter and punctuation. His poems are concerned with the vicissitudes of life. In tone, they can best be described as "mellow." Nimoy is a photographer, too, and his photos (a pair of mascara-ed eyes, autumn leaves swept across old stone steps, a junction of train tracks, blurry faces, long-haired lovers and the inevitable solitary man on a park bench) are interspersed among poems bearing such titles as "Daybreak and Darkness," "Seasons," "Joy and Sorrows," "In Places" and "At Times."

Nimoy cites as his stylistic influences Lawrence Ferlinghetti, Rod McKuen and E. E. Cummings and admires the work of Bob Dylan. "If I'm moved I'll write about anything, anywhere and time," he says. "I might be on a plane and may just pick up an American Airlines magazine, for example, and jot down a poem."

Celestial Arts recently published Nimoy's third book,

I Am Not Spock. As much as Nimoy dislikes being identified by the public solely as Mr. Spock, he admits it has
benefited his career as a poet. Nearly 300,000 copies of
You and I are in print, at least five times as many as any
single volume by a non-celebrity poet. "I know I'm very
lucky," admits the erstwhile TV alien. "Great American
poets don't have a market."

But Richard Harris, a leading celebrity poet, does. He
not only gives frequent TV recitations, but has won
Grammy awards for his recorded readings of *Jonathan Liv-
ingston Seagull* and Kahlil Gibran's *The Prophet*. A collection of his poems, *I, In The Membership of My Days*, has
recently been published by Random House. Harris, like
Nimoy, makes use of free verse and unique punctuation—
an ampersand, for example, where the actual conjunction
"and" might do. Following in the tradition of Sylvia Plath
and Ann Sexton, Harris's poetry is largely concerned with
the passage of time and death, as illustrated by such
macabre imagery as "purple pining mothers," "through
the dark corridors of their thighs," "In a sperm flush of
dust," "to rise and breed dead maggots in my brain" and
"too late in the lost sun."

Harris denies that his poetry bespeaks a certain bleak-
ness of life. "I write about anything, any time, any place,
anywhere," he asserts, reiterating an oft-espoused motto
of the celebrity poet. "I'm not influenced by anyone, but I
admire the work of Keats, Yeats and Manley Hopkins. But
one reviewer said my poetry was [Dylan] Thomasesque."

Preferring an intimacy offered only by vanity presses
and small gatherings of poetry buffs are George Reinholt,
star of daytime TV's "One Life to Live," and "Medical
Center" idol Chad Everett. Reinholt writes best when
"ticked off." His podium? George Reinholt fan clubs. Chad
Everett wrote a book of poetry, *A Toast to Shelby* (his
wife), published it himself, then touted it in an ad in
Rona Barrett's *Hollywood* magazine. "A book of personal

poetry composed by a man filled with love!" read the copy. "This is Chad Everett's first collection of poems in which he shares his innermost feelings about love and life. They reveal the warmth and strength of character that the media of television and movies just cannot capture." Everett's warmth and strength of character, however, were captured the night he appeared on the "Dick Cavett Show" and discussed the sonnets of Shakespeare, Auden and Chad Everett. (An Everett sampling: "Here's to those blue eyes/Those blue eyes/That are my strength and conversation.") *A Toast to Shelby*, alas, is no longer available —to the press, at least—because Everett, says his press agent, feels it was a crass mistake to sell his poetry through Miss Rona's unliterary review.

Celebrity poetry is a rich and multi-textured form and certainly deserves inclusion on the selective pages of *The New York Times Book Review, The New York Review of Books* and the *Paris Review.* Is the celebrity poet content to remain a mere cipher among his highly acclaimed poetic peers? As the great British poet Oliver Goldsmith observed, "Of all kinds of ambition, that which pursues poetical fame is the wildest."

GREAT
WRITERS

Pimento

Old food in the pantry, as it ages, sometimes acquires fungus. When that happens, it is possible, upon removing the lids, to smell in certain vessels the original food: a hint of sardine seeps through the botulism of a half-opened tin, a forgotten fruitcake yields potent memories despite a shroud of bacteria, the pimento jar of our lives, now covered with mold, no longer contains simply "pimento": it contains mold-covered pimento, a reminder of what happened when the pimento was new and what happened as the pimento grew old. I think it is significant to say that examining the original food, refashioned with the embellishments of age, is a way of smelling and then smelling again.

To reach into the jar of my past—that is all I wanted to do in this book. I've smelled what was there yesterday, what is there today, and—if Helen, the housekeeper, does not clear out the pantry soon—what will surely be there forever.

Tadpole

Dash was dead and I wasn't sleeping well. I used to wake up early in the morning, take walks, rummage around the house, think about my ridiculous and colorful Southern family. It was during one of these early-morning funks that my typewriter fell on my head and knocked me unconscious on the wooden floor that is the floor of my house that I walk on when I'm not elsewhere. Sometime later—I do not know how much later—I regained consciousness, reached out and embraced the goldfish bowl in front of me, and remembered our mismatched trio and the discussion that took place seven-and-a-half hours after the tadpole grew into a frog and died. I had said to Dash, "You are an amphibian, too. You knew what it meant when the tadpole grew into a frog and wanted to go home. You had rapport with the tadpole. Where do I fit in?"

Several days later, Dash said: "How should I know, Lily? I'm just a penny-a-line hack. What do I know about life?"

Those were wonderful years. Royalties from *The Tiny Weasels* enabled me to buy a house on the outskirts of Dingman's Falls, New York, at that time a fashionable— though not snobby—area. Dash was making money and we fixed up the house and lived off the land. Many people told me that the soil was no good, but, always a fighter, I told them all to go to hell and roast. I hired a fellow German, Heinz Boering, to help in my travails with the land, for I knew that the two of us together could force the land into submission and extract from it many delightful things. Heinz and I raised an impressive colony of heifers, sold them at an embarrassing profit, used the money to plant an orange grove, a grape orchard, apple trees, and a patch of brussels sprouts; sold those and bought wild quail, ate and sold and ate the quail; invented a new azalea hybrid; enriched the lake with freshwater bivalves; and revolutionized the parakeet industry. But that was before everything went bad and I was no longer welcome in Hollywood and neither was Dash, who went to jail.

My strongest memory of those years (though I'm not clear why) is of my encounter with the tadpole and the way it changed my life. It was near the lake one day with my pet poodle, Salaud, that I heard the first strange gurglings of springtime, peered into the murky liquid, and spotted what looked like an elongated and enlarged spermatozoon bounding along in a remarkably carefree manner. Evidently, Salaud had sensed my curiosity, for he barked loudly and ferociously, and it was quite a while, an hour perhaps (or maybe less), before I could calm him down. But I wanted to know more about this unusual squiggle of life that piqued the wonder of both me and Salaud, so I compulsively—(I have that strong an interest in life)—scooped it up with my bare hands, the kind of thing I always did, still do, often. It left a pungent smell—a trace of which I can still smell now, will smell tomorrow, will surely smell forever—and I placed it in a jar that I quickly filled with water from the lake. I hurried home to show this example of life to Dash, who was quite knowledgeable about such things and would be able to teach me about the aforesaid wondrous movement, now inside the jar.

"What is this, Dash?"

"It's a tadpole, Lily."

"What's a tadpole, Dash?"

"Tadpoles grow into frogs, Lily."

"Then I suppose you'll want to kill it, Dash."

"That's right, Lily. You will learn to like frog's legs, too."

I was against it from the start, but I trusted Dash in matters such as the human food chain. We kept the tadpole inside the jar in which I had originally placed it until it grew too large and then Dash took it out—I refused to participate in the deathwatch—and put it in another jar. He repeated this process several times until sometime later (I do not know how much later), the tadpole had indeed become a frog as Dash had said it would and it was time to kill it.

On the table on which the jar rested Dash had carefully placed the tools he would need: a special trowel for the actual killing, several types of paring knives, salt, pepper, the typescript of the murder scene from a forthcoming novel. Helen, who normally did not mind the slaughtering of the food we ate, upchucked as Dash lifted, without remark, the frog out of its jar. It was a large frog, bigger than Dash's fist it seemed, still seems, bigger, actually, than both of his fists put together. He gripped the frog in one hand and attempted to bring down the special trowel on the frog's head, but the frog, sensing what was going to happen to him, expertly wriggled free before the special trowel hit his head. It was apparent that he had bounded off the table and out of the house, for we noticed a faint trail of blood heading down the porch and toward the lake.

"You must have nicked him, Dash," I said.

"What do I know about such things, Lily?" he said.

Salaud picked up the scent immediately and sometime later—I cannot recall how much later—located the injured frog at the edge of the lake and called us to the site with his ferocious bark. The frog twitched several times, rolled over on its back, kicked up its legs (the legs we were to have eaten), and died. Dash agreed that this frog was an unusual frog and did not deserve to be cut up into frog's legs. He headed knowingly back to the house while I remained behind, wondering about humanity. Sometime later—how much later I do not know—I decided to bury the frog. The air was clammy. I dug a suitable grave. I placed the frog in it. I covered it up. I went home and asked Dash what we should have for dinner.

"A side of beef, Lily."

"Roasted or broiled, Dash?"

"Do what you want, Lily."

That was a hell of a way to talk, I thought, and it made, still makes, me angry. I left the house, got in the car, turned on the ignition and drove to the Canadian border. Four days later, perhaps five, I came back with the snuffles.

Silly Billy

"Lily, I need money to go kill some Indians down near Belize," said Silly Billy to my Aunt Lily (after whom I was named). Aunt Lily was a complex person who for reasons which have never been entirely clear frequently indulged the flamboyant requests of Silly Billy, who, when he was in town, was her husband. At least it appeared that way for a time. Silly Billy's request seemed odd, still seems odd, because it was issued during a picnic through Worcestershire, Aunt Lily's devoted Negro chauffeur, who sat between her and Silly Billy and acted, until the end, as the spokesman for both of them to each other.

"You haven't repaid the interest on the last loan," Aunt Lily replied by way of Worcestershire.

"It was too damned high," Silly Billy said.

"You haven't repaid the interest on the loan before that," Aunt Lily said.

"Aw, come on, Lily. Give a guy a break. I'll never ask for anything again. Maybe I'll even bring back some—" But the words were muffled because he put his hand over his mouth as he whispered to Worcestershire and Worcestershire followed suit when he relayed Silly Billy's message to Aunt Lily.

How strange, to a child, the secretiveness was. I had admired my Aunt Lily—been enchanted, enamored, by and of her—and loved to wander through her spacious closets and read the labels on clothes especially imported

from European ports-of-call. There had been little I did
not know about her, I thought at the time, until the incident at the picnic, which was, even to a remarkably per-
ceptive child like me, baffling.

Our slaves—(former slaves, actually, but they stayed
with the family for lack of any other sanctuary over the
years)—were the only household inhabitants who would
know why Silly Billy cupped his hand and whispered when
he gave Worcestershire a message for Aunt Lily. I asked
them to explain it.

"Them that does what they wants, gets what they wants,
in the sweet by and by," said Minnie May Jones with a
smile. Minnie May was my maid, and I always took,
still take (now that I reassess it), her smile to indicate ag-
gravation at the unworldliness of white people. I pressed
her further about the behavior of Silly Billy and Aunt Lily
and Worcestershire. Worcestershire, as it happened, was
Minnie May's half-brother and therefore likely (though
I'm not sure how likely) to confide in her.

"Y'all watch out fo' Silly Billy," Minnie May said. "He
up to no good."

"Then why is Aunt Lily married to Silly Billy?" I aksed.

"Swing low sweet Cadillac," murmured Minnie May.
"May Jesus bless dis chile wif a brain."

As I left the laundry room, I heard Minnie May cackling
to herself, a cackle, I later realized (no, I do not know
how much later) that was a profound and significant
cackle. I think it was when I returned to visit my ludicrous
mishmash of a family, possibly, that I found out what kind
of a man Silly Billy was (he was, among other things, the
source of the illegal "loco weed," as I'm told it is called,
that Aunt Lily stored in a sack that dangled between her
breasts and consumed whenever there was a full moon),
and why Minnie May smiled each time I broached the
subject of Silly Billy and Worcestershire.

But by then it was too late, for I was hopelessly in love

with Silly Billy. Having just returned from a Central American adventure (surely an ignominious one, but I was blind, as the young often are; God help the immature in their single-minded passions and stubbornly noble refusal and inability to recognize the ugliness of life), Silly Billy entertained us at dinner with tales of wheeling and dealing. These were, alas, the sort of stories that always made, still make, easy prey out of me; Dash knew it, I knew it, and together we had argued drunkenly about it. But sometimes, though I'm not sure how many times, I was—(still am?)—a creature of libido, like any sensitive pre-adult. Later that night (perhaps it was the next night; my memories of those years are so disjointed), Silly Billy yanked my arm crudely, dragged me out to the terrace, and said: "Whad'ya say we go bag some possums, kid?"

I have often wondered why I did not display more ebullience at this request, such as by exclaiming "Holy Toledo" or another similar acknowledgment of joy, for that was without a doubt how I felt: joyful. What I did, before Silly Billy had time to load his rifle and borrow more money from Aunt Lily, was to get into the front seat of the shiny, new car Aunt Lily had recently purchased for him. Then, Silly Billy and I drove to a swamp where he sent up strange signals: smoke signals, whistle signals, and finally signals of shouting and screaming. I thought, wanted to think, that perhaps this was a prelude to some sort of wild passion. I remember smelling something acrid —eucalyptus oil possibly, ochre—I do not know. A Cajun waif in a torn dress stumbled out from behind a cyprus tree. Silly Billy spanked the Cajun for a long time (my guess is three-and-a-half hours, but it might have been more). I ran—trudged, actually: one cannot run through swamp mud—to the car and waited.

"Now I know about murderers and bad men," I said the next day to Dash in Hollywood.

"What makes you think so, Lily?"

That was a hell of a way to talk, I thought, and it made, still makes, me angry. I left the house, got in the car, turned on the ignition and drove to the Canadian border. Four days later, perhaps five, I came back with the flu.

Bertha

"Dear Southern Relative," the letter said, says now, will say tomorrow (unless it is destroyed), "Bertha will be departing Brooklyn sometime between January 1 and June 31, depending on when the train strike is over. They say it will be over soon, and we hope and pray that it is. Rest assured, dear wealthy relation, that we fully trust your intentions and know that you will provide Bertha with clothing and roughage and other things that we, alack, cannot. How distant Lake Pontchartrain sounds to us (is that where you live, or hunt?); it is as if our daughter were journeying to Khartoum. Yet we hope and pray every night and every day that we will live to flee Brooklyn and meet with you and your family, the blessed and well-fed members of our tree."

The letter was, still is, addressed to Sidney Freeman, my grandfather, who arranged for Bertha to marry Luke Goldberg, a cousin and therefore (though I'm not exactly sure how) a distant relation to me. Luke, I learned through a slip-up in the passing on of the family diaries, was an embarrassment to the family: he gambled frivolously, he wrote bad checks, he was something of a gigolo, and he frequently molested children. By marrying him off to Bertha, a relative, it was hoped that Luke would settle down and cease causing the family to somersault in unison whenever his name was brought up in front of company. But approximately three hours after the marriage, Luke ran off with a shrimp-canning heiress from Johnson's Bayou and Bertha, now a deserted wife, moved in with the two sisters, my absurd great-aunts, Lucretia and Letitia Shapiro.

I met Bertha when I was a child and my first memories of her are, as are all childhood memories, childlike. I remember her as being awfully tall and exotic. It wasn't until much later—though exactly how much later I do not know—that I realized she was neither tall nor exotic and was in fact somewhat squat and ordinary. I think this had something to do with a snapshot of Bertha I discovered accidentally among the mementos of Casselle Finkelstein, my third cousin by an early (and not talked-about) marriage of Aunt Mary Lou Leibowitz to a local ne'er-do-well, apparently.

But such are the vagaries of childhood and I do not regret what I have since realized was a crush that I had on Bertha because it was through my infatuation with her that I learned one of the great lessons of my life. Bertha had a curious habit of disappearing at lunchtime from the home of whichever unusual relation had consented to keep her at the time. Whenever she returned, I called her to my bedroom where I told her about the books I was reading: Proust, Flaubert, Euclid, Baudelaire, Swift—I was an exceptionally bright child and there were few people with whom I could discuss my reading habits. Certainly I could not discuss them with my mother, who at that time read only Rosicrucian tracts (later, there were other religions); nor could I do so with my father, a busy, though smart, man. Bertha, of course, was not genuinely interested in my literary discussions, but I did not know that at the time, and had I known, it would have been of little consequence, for I was quite taken with her and the mysterious, alluring phonetics of her Brooklyn accent. But it was when she started to miss my mid-afternoon literary salon, I think, that I began to wonder with whom Bertha was lunching and imagined the kinds of things that only a child's mind can imagine.

One day I followed Bertha on one of her lunchtime excursions. She walked through town past rows of robust Creole vendors. I lost her somewhere in the French Quarter. I peeked between the hanging *saucissons*, lifted up half-dead lobsters, searched behind mountains of garlic cloves, but Bertha was not there and therefore her whereabouts became even more appealing to me. I didn't want to do it, but I was irretrievably drawn to a knowledgeable-looking peddler and before I could weigh the consequences, I had uttered: *"Excusez-moi, monsieur. Est-ce que vous connaissez* Bertha?"

He blanched and hurriedly trundled off. I queried another peddler; his pleasant demeanor immediately soured and it wasn't until many peddlers later—although I'm not certain how many peddlers later—that I was given a functional clue.

"Ovair zaire," the peddler said, in the patois of the Franco-American community of the southern states. He pointed toward a nondescript shack.

The sign said, says now, and probably will not say tomorrow, as the area has gone bad and is being torn down, "Johnny-Bob's Bagel Noshery." It was hand-lettered on a crudely fashioned blackboard slate and was partly obscured by ambitious platters of food stacked haphazardly on the windowsill. My mind took note of the kind of detail other writers have never noticed (or—at least—reported): why was there no shellfish, for example, in this store, when all other stores in Bogalusa were well-stocked with shellfish? It was a cruel answer that I was to learn only with the passing of time.

What seemed like hours passed—but I am sure it was only seconds—before I realized that Bertha was seated at one of the back tables across from a handsome fellow with dark hair and an apron. They held hands tensely. I crouched down beneath the sign's edge between the place where the window stopped—or began, I'm not sure which —and stared longingly at Bertha and her handsome lunch-time beau. After many exchanged glances, they pressed their faces together at an angle enabling their lips to touch (although I could not see their lips, I am certain their lips were touching), and they held this position for some time. Then they drew apart, gazed at each other, and re-sumed this position at the opposite angle. They main-tained this mode of touching for a very long time, an hour perhaps.

I tried explaining what this meant to me years later—I must say, I am not sure exactly how many years later—to Dash over drinks. I tried explaining this, along with the fact that Bertha was in Johnny-Bob's Bagel Noshery every day at lunchtime because she wanted to go home like everyone else and that was why I had just ordered a truckload of Hellmann's mayonnaise.

"I don't get it, Lily," Dash said. "What do I know about life?"

That was a hell of a way to talk, I thought, and it made, still makes, me angry. I left the house, got in the car, turned on the ignition and drove to the Canadian border. Four days later, perhaps five, I came back with pneu-monia.

Lunch at Lamston's

This all happened after the war in Vietnam. I was heading downtown after a taping of the Cheap Show, on which the marvelously spunky MISS JILL ST. JOHN and I are fellow celebrity panelists, to meet my long-time friend and confidante POPPY ARMSWORTH. Poppy is the heiress to the sinfully bottomless fire-hose fortune, amassed by her great-grandfather on her mother's side—a driver of hard bargains and descendant of Wilmot Proviso. Talk about style! This country hasn't produced anyone appealing since TEDDY ROOSEVELT's trust-busting days and I find it all disheartening. That's what I like about Poppy, I suppose; she knows she's dead-end and doesn't apologize for it. Still, it's dismaying to report that Poppy has frittered away all of the interest and a good deal of the capital itself, and has now taken to putting her name on the bottoms of jeans and selling them through cheesy outlets around town in order to pay for her next DERMO-PLASTY.

Gliding through Sheridan Square to our rendezvous at the wonderfully tacky Quiche and Brew, part of that new nationwide chain of fast-food *caffès* so popular with the brunch bunch, I found myself inexorably drawn across SEVENTH AVENUE to Christopher Street where I lived so many years ago. Still do live there, in fact, at least I

think I do. When did JUDY GARLAND die? Because I
went to Judy's funeral and that was the same day the ken-
nel delivered MAGGIE, and I seem to have trouble pic-
turing her anywhere but *downtown.*

There were the familiar aspidistra stores, the novelty
shops selling ashtrays that look like cigarettes, those little
leather boutiques, the two queues for Häagen-Dazs (one
chocolate, one vanilla)—it was a scene that gently trans-
ported me back to a kind of euphoria I thought had died
along with the last Broadway run of *Hello, Dolly.* Wander-
ing aimlessly, forgetting my appointment with Poppy
(who had probably stopped in Washington Square Park
to watch Negroes play instruments), I somehow ended up
in front of a place called, simply enough, Xerox and Yesterday. It was one of those antique shops, but hardly anyone ever buys antiques because they're too expensive. So:
they also have a convenient photocopying service and all
the playwrights in the neighborhood like it because the
Xerox machine is hidden in the armoire so they can pre-
tend they're *really* shopping for antiques when—

"TR-UU!" a voice called out.

And *there* was STEVE RUBELLA, proprietor of New
York's poshest discotheque and host to so many of my
dearest FRIENDS. "Tru, I've been trying you all *day*," he
said, agitatedly. "All I get is the damn SERVICE."

Somewhat miffed, I replied, "You should have left a
message. I check in every hour." I hoped the girls weren't
fouling up again.

"I couldn't," Steve said. "The girl kept asking why she
couldn't get into the club last night."

"Just how exclusive *is* it if the people who answer other
people's telephones are trying to get in?" I countered.
"And what's that green pomade all over your priceless
ART DECO shirt sleeves?"

"God. I was so busy trying to find you that I just didn't
have time to change. MICK JAGGER came in last night

and had a hay fever attack. At least he said it was hay
fever, but I think he's got one of those SEPTUM PROB-
LEMS, but that's just between you and me, and ANDY,
okay? I hear LIZA has one, too. Mick didn't have a hand-
kerchief and he was sneezing all over the place so I held
out my arm and said, 'Here, Mick. Sneeze on this. It's
only MONEY.' So he did. Can you believe it? MICK
JAGGER sneezed on *my arm*, the arm of this refreshingly
pushy little Jewish guy from Long Island—"

"Steve," I replied, "was that why you've been trying to
touch base? As my AGENT loves to say?"

"Oh Jesus Christ, Tru, of course not." He reached into
his inside pocket and withdrew a newspaper clipping.
"Have you seen this?" he asked, unfolding a recent "Suzy
Says." SUZY is positively my all-time favorite historian.
Why, a day without Suzy is like a day without . . . oh
heavens . . . like a day without . . . oh, I don't know.
Where did JACK hide that vermouth? All I can say is that
Suzy Knickerbocker is like mother's milk to me and that's
all there is to it.

"Dateline *Calcutta*. Pay attention, freedom fans; eternal
vigilance is the price of democracy, or some such. Last
week at the luxe new Calcutta Arms, one of *our* boys—I
won't tell you which, and wouldn't even for all the oolong
in the dazzling People's Republic—caused an international
scandale (that's scandal to anyone reading this in the subway) when he donned a silk sari and caste appliqué and
swept into the Louis Seize dining room as—who else?—*La
Gandhi*. Personally, I'm writing a letter to the editor. How
about you?"

Dear. How in heaven's name could I describe the effect
this item had on me? The impersonator in question was,
without doubt, MR. WALLY GONIGHTLY. I have
tried for months to get Mr. Gonightly out of my mind,
yet whenever I am close to purging this particular memory, something happens to recall him once again. The

scent of Viennese roast, the doorman at BENDEL'S, blue
jellybean sandals—so many things the two of us shared, so
many things impossible to avoid now. . . .

I am, I admit, an impressionable person. Whenever my
pencil approaches the pages of my little Blue Jay copy-
books (or is that what TENNESSEE WILLIAMS uses? I
was never quite sure), I somehow begin thinking about
MISS ROYAL HOLLISTER, who cared for me for just
about as long as I can remember.

"It's time to be nice to our neighbors," she would an-
nounce every year as the holidays approached. I always
did what she said, first of all because she was old, and
second of all because she dressed funny. But most of all I
knew that some day my dreamlike recollections of Southern boyhood would permit me to meet wonderful people
like ELEANOR and FRANK PERRY. Miss Hollister
made me invite for dinner people with names like Little
Daddy and Muskrat because that was her way. I never
quite fancied these get-togethers (they seemed so forced),
but today, her passion to entertain is, like her recipe for
brandied fruitcake, something I carry always in my heart
of hearts.

"Li'l Buddy," I can hear her saying, "I reckon you didn't
much enjoy dinner tonight but from it you have learnt an
important lesson. You must always remember the value
of gala events. If God had wanted life to be boring, he
wouldn't have made Dixie cups. But do not forsake your
mission to record your view of the world. You will know
this has happened when you have been a guest on the
JOHNNY CARSON SHOW 312 times."

I remember the day Wally Gonightly arrived at my
building on Christopher Street. I lived on the second floor
above the superintendent, a Japanese who bore an
uncanny resemblance to MICKEY ROONEY, and was re-

warding myself with an expresso for thinking about working on my novel when suddenly my buzzer rang, not once, not twice, not three times, not four times, but a good ten or twelve times. I opened my door and ran downstairs to look into the commotion.

"Oh, Mr. C.," a man at the bottom of the stairs trilled through the vestibule door. I use man advisedly, by the way, for the person at the bottom of the stairs was dressed, or dressed up, to be precise, exactly like AUDREY HEPBURN. This was no half-baked imitation; it was simply perfect, right down to the shiny gloss of that marvelous period lipstick, Cherries in the Snow. The man was stomping his foot and demanding I let him in. We discussed the matter on the front steps, which have a delightful history all their own, being the scene of many twilight quarrels with ever-so-many beaux.

"Mr. C., you've just got to let me move into this building! Some boys dream about growing up to be a baseball player or fireman. But ever since I was two, I knew I was different. That's when I started dreaming about KEELEY SMITH."

How charming this visitor was, how positively disarming. I vowed then and there to become his lifelong fan, his temporarily faithful helpmate, his brunch companion, relishing this new excuse not to expand my magazine excerpt of a novel into a full-length manuscript.

"I'm Mr. Wally Gonightly," he said, handing me a calling card with his name engraved in silver glitter, and underneath, in the corner, *Cruising*. He appropriated a mailbox, then proceeded to install a full-size make-up mirror with lights ("to check my mascara before making an excursion to Lamston's," he explained. "Which, of course, is something I've always wanted to do"). I promptly took his bags upstairs.

"Love that RETRO LOOK, don't you?" Wally said. His set of World War II luggage was overflowing with the most exquisite antique outfits. "I've visited every thrift shop you can name," he continued, "and—do I have a wardrobe or do I—" I had to admit that he *did* have a wardrobe. HARLOW in *Dinner at Eight*, HEPBURN & Poitier in *Guess Who's Coming to Dinner?*, JILL CLAY-BURGH in *An Unmarried Woman*—Wally could change into any of these extraordinary women at a moment's notice. His furniture arrived the next day and it, too, was a tribute to those wonderful days when men were men and women were women and the rich threw those flagrantly lavish parties. I took inventory and here's what I saw: one Deco dressing table with a blue-tinted mirror shaped like a swan, a collection of FIESTAWARE for thirty-five, two HOWDY DOODY lunchboxes ("I used to take one to school," Wally said sweetly), a JAYNE MANSFIELD bath towel set, an early EISENHOWER dinette, deck chairs from the OLD Normandie, a Liber-typhone, a Horn & Hardart baked beans bowl, a fox stole ZELDA FITZGERALD once wore into a pool, and every DINAH SHORE album ever recorded.

Wally and I became very close. One afternoon he knocked on my door, apparently having just wakened because his BALENCIAGA sleeping goggles were still draped around his neck. "Know-ez vous what day it is?" he inquired. "TUESDAY. That means the dime store is having its weekly shrimp RIOT. I do hope you'll join me," he continued, "for lunch at Lamston's."

Somewhat miffed, I replied: "I am busy. Have you seen my pink index cards?"

"Oh, Tru! *Quel killjoy!* Lamston's is so the pits—a statement, yes? About modern American life, don't you think? Besides, I've always wanted to sample their jumbo shrimp. I hear it's revolting. Where is your *joie de vivre*, your *nostalgie de la bouef*? It's RESEARCH."

How could I resist Wally's primitive charm? We cabbed right over to the Sixth Avenue dime store, though

I wasn't planning to eat as I really cannot accommodate any food the consuming of which requires taking big bites. Do you know what I mean? Somehow, there's nothing like a good banana curry to make you feel like you are in the ORIENT eating baby food.

When we arrived, Wally drew my attention to a sign in the window which read "Try Our Raft-'O'-Frankfurters Today! You'll Love it!" "El tacko," Wally swooned. Inside, while he consumed his seafood platter rather elegantly, I busied myself in the trim-a-tree department. (I must admit that the ham sandwich supreme looked tempting, but the help refused to cut it into triangles, so I said never you mind.) It was only natural for all those dime-store trinkets to remind me of another time, another place, another person I no longer am, and never will be again. Will I ever be able to look at a household decoration without thinking of Miss Royal Hollister? With the exception of JACK D., she paid more attention to me than anyone else in my whole life. "Li'l Person," I can hear her saying, "some folks aren't lucky as you. They don't have odd relatives with an antebellum past who can teach them how to allegory."

On the way home, Wally confessed that this excursion to Lamston's was the "time of his life" and carried on about how "we must come back again to try the ind. can tuna w/slaw." Next to my masked ball in 1968 and that marvelous IRISH CATHOLIC PIPE-FITTER whose entire family I seduced, I had to agree that this was a most unusual adventure.

Several weeks later, I heard Wally singing out on the fire escape. He was singing the disco version of "Moon River." How naive and simple he now seemed; he was, after all, just a cute country boy of whom I had evidently grown quite fond. "That's beautiful," I said, leaning out the bay-style window with the *crepe de chine* drapes.

"I shouldn't let myself go that way," he answered. "*Voulez-vous* come upstairs and have a chat *avec moi?*"

As I made myself comfortable in one of Wally's invaluable DECK CHAIRS (c. 1942), he said, "Tru, I think I'm ready for New York. But," he pondered, "is New York ready for me?"

"In other words," I surmised, a bit weary of the endless veiled requests that come my way, but intrigued, nonetheless, "you'd like me to invite thousands of my dearest FRIENDS to a party at which you make your debut."

"*Oui.*"

"You'll have to do something about those dreadful Gallicisms," I pointed out. "*Capisci?*"

Still and all, I agreed to arrange the festivities, take care of the guest list, the catering, all those last-minute little extras which can send even the most accomplished hostess to COLUMBIA PRESBYTERIAN for months of recovery.

Then we spent hours discussing how Wally should make his debut. "You know," he said, "drag queens in New York City are a dime a dozen. I can do a devastating CAROL CHANNING, and everyone agrees my ELLA FITZGERALD is *magnifique*, but that doesn't really make me a star, does it?"

Well, I was the first to admit that New York society needed someone like Wally to give it new shine and sparkle; it really hadn't been the same since CALVIN KLEIN and that ugly DOMINICAN affair.

The party was scheduled for later that year, in October, to make sure everyone would be back from the Hamptons in time for Wally's arrival. I hired a Mack truck and parked it near the wharves under the West Side Highway. The invitations read: "You are quietly urged by the man who might embarrass you in his forthcoming book to attend a gala event honoring his favorite person at this very moment, Mr. Wally Gonightly. At the desig-

nated time, please head directly to The Spike, and look
for the distinctive big truck painted Freuhauf yellow.
Representatives of DEFUNCT European and Middle-
Eastern MONARCHIES have promised to attend."

It was the event of the season. The buffet table (by
Lamston's, naturally) groaned under the weight of all the
grilled cheese sandwiches (I paid extra to have them cut
into those tiny, bite-size triangles), fountain delights, fruit
medleys, vegetable symphonies, fish cakes and spaghetti,
veal cordon bleue [sic], beef 'n' peach plates, piping hot
tuna melts, soup de jour, fresh-baked donuts, and bottomless cups of coffee.

And, I am pleased to report, all of my FAVORITE
PEOPLE attended. (Imagine my embarrassment if they
had gone instead to the BILL BRADLEY fund-raiser, an
event with which I was competing that very night?) Well,
as Miss Royal Hollister always said, thank your lucky stars
for all of those other voices in all of those other rooms.
JACKIE was there, so was LEE, and even poor EDIE
BEALE (whose recent engagement at RENO SWEE-
NEY'S was not to be missed). Of course, there was
ANDY, BIANCA, LIZA, JUDY, YVES, HALSTON, LOU-
LOU DE LA FALAISE, LOLA FALANA, LOUISE
LASSER, GEORGE STEINBRENNER, VITAS GERU-
LAITIS, ALLEN GINSBERG, JOAN CRAWFORD'S
SHOES, the handsome SHERIFF I interviewed for . . .
for . . . hell, what was the name of my last book? The
one about those BAD PEOPLE in Kansas? Oh yes, THE
CRONKITES were there, and so was HUGH CAREY,
ANNE FORD, RABBI KORFF, PEARL BAILEY, TENG
XIAOPING, JERRY LEWIS, ROY COHN (impeccably
dressed, as always), ALTOVISE DAVIS, GORDON
LIDDY, ANTONIO SOMOZA, GENERAL TORRIJOS,
RUPERT MURDOCH, MARTIN BORMANN, HENRY
KISSINGER—and then the SHAH phoned to apologize
for not attending (he said he was "busy taping a Holly-

wood Squares") but that if HELMUT wanted to use his old jails for a photo location in his next book, *Colored Women,* he was more than welcome, provided of course, that the Shah ever got back from vacation. I don't see why people don't like the Shah. If Helmut had wanted an American jail, would any warden have been gracious enough to allow the use of one, even while the inmates were dining?

Wally could not have been more magnificent: arriving two hours late as the former First Lady, BETTY FORD, and flanked by an entourage of "reporters."

"Mrs. Ford, what would you do if your daughter were having an affair?"

"Well, I wouldn't be surprised . . ."

"Mrs. Ford, do you and your husband sleep together?"

"Well, I wouldn't be surprised . . ."

"Mrs. Ford, do you have a pill problem?"

"Well, I wouldn't be surprised . . ."

"Mrs. Ford, have you had a face lift?"

"Well, I wouldn't be surprised . . ."

It was a masterful tribute to one of America's most delightful ladies, and Wally spent the next quarter hour happily dispensing beauty tips. At the end of the evening, it could truly be said that Wally had become a permanent chandelier in the New York salon.

That, however, was the last I would see of him. The next day, as I was heading out for Medaglia d'Oro, I came across a note taped to my door. *"Au revoir,"* it said, "you can keep my Dinah Shores."

I hoped Wally would post me a line as soon as he arrived wherever it was that he was going, but he never did. It was just like the time he "accidentally" burnt two cigarette HOLES in my red silk dinner jacket (a favorite piece of *Chinoiserie*—yes, in this case, French is perfectly acceptable). He never BOTHERED to replace it. Still,

one is supposed to make allowances for tortured souls
such as MISTER Wally Gonightly. Months later, I ran
into Steve Rubella; Suzy's column made Wally sound very
happy, but then that was Suzy's specialty. And, yes,
Wally's coming-out party was a smashing success. In fact,
my FRIENDS want me to have another one—can you believe it? They don't think I'm ever going to finish *Answered . . . Answered . . . Answered Machine?* That
novel I'm working on! My housemate still keeps the vermouth out of reach, but I have some new hiding places
even Jack DOESN'T KNOW ABOUT. Well. Tomorrow
I'll talk the whole thing over with POPPY. We're having
brunch. 1:00 P.M. Quiche and Brew. *I'll* be there, anyway.

The Joan Didion Album

The Day the Sixties Ended

There had been something in the air. I am not sure exactly what. I remember going outside and noting signs
of change. There was a rattlesnake in the bougainvillaea.
There was no lingering fragrance of jasmine, which
meant that the night-blooming jasmine had decided not
to open up the night before. The car had been backed
into the garage, instead of driven straight in. The mail
was late, and I felt an urge to sift through letters—I did
not care whose address they bore or whether they had
been written by people or computers. The lounge chairs
around the pool were folded: a rejection. I went inside.
Why not? There were more signs of change, although I
did not know at the time exactly what was to change.
There were no leftovers from the night before. That
seemed strange. I could not remember the guests finish-
ing everything. I could remember filling containers of
varying shapes with food and carefully covering each one
with Reynold's Wrap. After we had the framboise, I put
everything in the refrigerator. But it was not there now.
There should have been half a wheel of Brie. There
should have been the remainders of a smoked mozzarella

and basil and tomato salad. There should have been an entire vegetable terrine.

I went back outside. I decided to open up one of the lounge chairs. It was the kind that had perforated slats and after I sat on it for a while, I got up and there were big red welts across my thighs. I knew that was because I had sat in one position too long, but I have a tendency to do that. I turned on the radio and it was tuned to the all-news station. That's the only one I listen to except when I am in my car searching for a particular frequency which goes with freeway driving. I can never find one, so I generally end up turning the radio off. But this day I needed some sort of noise, a few words, some static, which would put me in touch with whatever it was that everyone else seemed to be in touch with. Only the all-news station can do that, although not in the expected way. I do not listen to the headlines; I tune in for the monotone of an excited voice rattling off news of catastrophes. I arranged a towel on the lounge chair so I would not get welts, and sat down again. I remember blanking out for a long time and then coming to as the voice on the radio said that Jerry Rubin had gotten his hair cut. When I heard this item of news, I wondered about several things. I wondered about Jerry Rubin's barber, and if he understood the significance of his job. I wondered about Jerry Rubin, and whether or not this haircut was a spur-of-the-moment thing. Most of all, I wondered about me. If I had been there to witness Jerry Rubin getting his hair cut, would I have heard the Sixties falling to the floor? I got up and there was the imprint of terrycloth across my thighs. And then I went inside and told my husband about what the voice on the radio had said and the really astonishing thing was this: We were not surprised.

·

Sometime in the Middle of the Seventies

Occasionally, when I am in an airplane wearing a cash-
mere sweater and wool skirt and it is still cold enough for
an American Airlines blanket, I wonder about the following: Am I a representative of an era, and if so, which
one is it? I think about how I went to college in the 1950s.
To some, this means that I am a member of the Beat Generation. To others, it means that I liked Ike. I might have
liked Ike. I don't know. Once, somebody asked me if I was
silent in the Fifties. What did I think of the Hollywood
blacklist? they wanted to know. I have thought about
these questions a lot. I don't have the answers. What I do
have is the memory that the Fifties were a time when
people played bongos and flutes and smoked something
called reefer, which I had always thought was a variety of
ladies' coat. I think it was at Berkeley that I had my first
experience with Jane Bowles, the meaning of the blank
page, and black saxophone players. All of this was somehow connected with the first time I smoked marijuana,
and I remember sitting on a cold surface somewhere,
putting my lips to a reefer and sucking and deciding that
the elements of this experience must mean something, and
that years later I would piece them all together: the
smoke, the strange, comforting coolness of the floor, the
perception that jazz would lead to rock and one day suburban children would live on crash-pad floors and a poet
named Bob Dylan would go electric and change the
course of music and because I am uninterested in rock
and roll, or any other form of music, I would get an assignment to interpret Jim Morrison. The most important
thing about the Jim Morrison interview was this: I sat
on a cold vinyl floor in his recording studio and realized
that I was not part of this, or any other, scene. Perhaps

that explained why, in 1964, I voted for Barry Goldwater. Perhaps that's why I am generally too weary to think of anything but brisk, cynical statements about things which are of major import to people with crushed linen clothing who reside in the large coastal cities. I recount these feelings so that I may be able to get up tomorrow morning and decide which era, if any, I represent.

The Day the Eighties Began

I have a propensity for malaise. It has struck me over the years without warning and for seemingly no reason at all. Or maybe there is always a warning and a reason. Or maybe there are several warnings and reasons. I don't know. What I do know is that this malaise, as I now analyze it, is predictable, like seasons. It generally strikes me on a day like this: I decide that I do not have a favorite color and cannot remember if I ever had one; my husband decides to have his next nervous breakdown in Atlantic City but not before he writes a magazine column about the modern Irish Catholic dilemma; my daughter decides that she does not like her name; my agent telephones to ask if I am interested in doing the rewrite on a screenplay that was ill-conceived to begin with, and I start wondering if there are any anagrams for the word *deal;* the Santa Ana winds which sweep in from the desert and wash across your mind like an airstream from a laundromat dryer are two hours late; I notice that the upholsterer did not sew the seams on my refurbished hunter-green couch correctly; a headline in a popular journal of the day tells me that shortages of everything are on the way; my early-model Corvette sits in the garage like a manifestation of the conceptual diamond lane; and

I have dinner at a shopping mall because it seems like the only thing left to do.

Today, the day the Eighties began, the malaise swept through my body with a ferocity I had not known before. I do not generally associate this malaise with the beginnings of decades, and so I have no idea why I felt it more strongly on this particular day than on any others. Usually there is only one thing I can do to defend myself against the malaise. Actually there are two things. During one of these onslaughts, I once wrote an article about how self-indulgent Woody Allen is. After slipping the carefully typed pages of Corrasable bond paper into an 8½×11-inch envelope and addressing it to the New York Review of Books, 250 W. 57th St., New York City, NY 10023, I felt energetic enough to visit Brooke Hayward. We discussed the emptiness of life in Los Angeles, the tedium of life on the other coast, and where else was there to go?

What I generally do when this malaise permeates my body is to go out behind my house, sit down on the cold stone patio—I like cold surfaces—and stare at my swimming pool. Sometimes, depending on whether or not there is a drought in Southern California, the water level is higher than others. Sometimes there are little water beetles floating on the surface. Sometimes there are leaves. Sometimes a slight breeze disturbs the water, and sometimes the water remains still, altered only by the reflection of an occasional cumulocirrus cloud formation floating over the Santa Monica Mountains. Sometimes the water filter comes on and makes noise.

More than the pool itself, I am fond of the tiles. The tiles in my pool display scenes of a fishing village in Portugal. It often happens as I am cruising the Hollywood Fwy trying to pay attention to signs that say *Franklin 1   La-Brea ½   San Vicente ¼* in order to get off at the proper exit, I find myself thinking of the tiles in my swimming pool. When that happens, I cannot get the picture out of my mind. And then I end up on the Pacific Coast Hwy, heading north, next exit, Mendocino. When I think about the tiles, I think about this: the people who made them, what made the people think of Portugal, why I felt that I had to have the tiles when I saw them in the swimming pool fixture store on Melrose, and the pattern of the tile arrangement—who thought of it, my architect or the workmen at the pool?

On the day the Eighties began, I was not at home. I was on the road, thinking about the tiles. Actually I was at home, in the morning. But later that day, I decided to drive to a hardware store to buy a new garden hose. We did not really need a new garden hose. But I decided to buy a new garden hose anyway: There was nothing else to do except go out and shop for garden hoses. On the way to the hardware store, I kept thinking about the tiles, and then a billboard I had seen earlier on the highway reappeared in my thoughts: Happy New Year. It was then that the malaise came over me, and I was not near my swimming pool. But that was all right. It was all right because of the following: I have been known to stare at my neighbor's swimming pool, when I have to. I have been known to stare at a hotel swimming pool when I have to. I have been known to stare at a picture of my swimming pool that I keep in my wallet next to my emergency medical identification, which I have made it a point to carry ever since the day years ago that I fainted in a parking lot. The diagnosis was acute malaise. I rejected the diagnosis, with a great deal of conviction, and they told me they were surprised that someone as tiny and frail as I am could get so angry. But I knew that my blackout had more to do with the fact that last week's *TV Guide* listed "Bonanza" at the wrong time, and I missed it, than with acute malaise.

Staring at the picture of the swimming pool that day

ameliorated the malaise, slightly. But the staring had not yet become a regimen for easing this feeling, and perhaps the staring must be done for a period of decades, sequentially, in order for it to work. I don't know. One thing I do know is that the actual act of swimming does not work. I never go in the swimming pool when affected by the malaise because it seems so sad that there are those deluded enough to believe that immersion of the individual in a body of flowing molecules can really make any difference in the general scheme of things. Mark Spitz's record-setting journey across an Olympic-sized hole in the ground has not yet changed anything. The ritual swim of religious pilgrims in the Ganges does not seem to have changed anything. Those bodies in the mud at Woodstock did not change anything. I tell you this not only as a way of assigning order to my life, but as a modern parable. The corollary is that the malaise that struck on the day the Eighties began has not yet receded, and I am sitting on a cold surface, thinking about sending out for sushi, as I piece together this perception.

THAT'S
ENTERTAINMENT

WHEN ETHNIC GROUPS arrive and settle in America, they enter the mainstream in various ways. Among the most prominent ways are boxing (they fight their way in) and stand-up comedy (they joke their way in). Each new wave of immigrants has produced its share of famous boxers and comedians. Here, then, is Henny Duc Tho, and . . .

The Monologue of the
First Vietnamese
Stand-up Comedian

Thank you, thank you. This is a wonderful club, you're fabulous people, and I'm lucky to be here. . . . Frankly, I'm lucky to be anywhere.

But seriously . . . waiter, could I have a drink? Thank you. Hey, I know. I need booze like Vietnam needs Cool Whip. Right? Listen, folks, I'm gonna let you in on a little secret. I always make it a practice never to drink before midnight. Fortunately, it happens to be midnight in Hanoi. . . . You know, last week I got so loaded they made me use the freight elevator. . . . Then there was the other night. I came home, stumbled into bed, and told my wife I loved her. She said, "Honey, are you drunk?" I said, "No, I'm having a napalm flashback."

Folks, I'm kidding. My wife's a beautiful person. Even though she can't keep house. Junk all over the place. At my house, we don't have spring cleaning, we have a spring offensive! Listen, my place is so dangerous you need a mine sweeper to find dinner! And the bathroom—my shower is so greasy it looks like the Gulf of Haiphong after a tanker spill. . . . Life is tough, folks. But not as tough as you think. You think things were tough in Flatbush? Back in Da Nang, things were so tough that my high school principal was named Bad Dog Bark. . . . He was a German shepherd.

You know, they say Vietnam is a land of equality. It's true. The rich people are running farms, peasants are writing books—and I headed for Thailand as soon as I got my driver's license. . . . But the other day I read that things are loosening up. The People's Press started a letters-to-the-editor column. They publish anything—but you have to give your name, address, and next of kin.

Listen, folks, there's a lot of poverty in Vietnam. Even the birds are economizing. They don't fly south for the winter—they take the bus. And things are happening fast. Too fast. You know, before the war, we had the Ho Chi Minh Trail. Now it's the Ho Chi Minh Expressway. It's even got a diamond lane for party workers who commute. Only they don't call it the diamond lane, they call it the mineral lane. Diamonds are too bourgeois. . . . Hey, am I talking to a rice painting, or what?

Hey, I like it here in America, but you know what I really miss? I miss Saigon. I miss the hustle and bustle, the hurly-burly, the nitty-gritty—but most of all I miss the cheap smack! But business is bad in Saigon. There used to be a nightclub on every corner. Today there's only one— and that's where the guy from *The Deer Hunter* is playing Russian roulette!

But seriously, folks, you gotta hand it to a country that's trying to rebuild itself after spending twenty years as the world's welcome mat! You know, Vietnam has some really heavy problems. I'm not kidding. I'm as serious as I have ever been in my entire life. I'm gonna say something I really want you to think about. You heard about a problem Vietnam is having with a chemical called Agent Orange. Folks, there's good news and bad news about Agent Orange. The good news is that my mother-in-law lived in a village that was completely decimated by Agent Orange. The bad news is that she was the only person to fully recover!

So, you win some and you lose some. . . . Am I right? Hey, is the egg roll greasy? Speaking of winners and losers, I wanna talk to you about some incredible winners— my pals, the boat people. In fact, the president of the boat people chapter of my fan club is here tonight. He's the guy doing all of the heckling. But that's okay—I know where his shrimp nets are! Just kidding, Tran. That's his name. Tran Van Sanh. His parents wanted something easy to remember. That's a joke, Tran. Folks, my buddy Tran is an excitable type. Turns everything into a Pueblo incident. . . . But people, about these wonderful human beings, the boat people. I wanna leave you with one thought tonight. Life is a demilitarized zone, defoliation rhymes with radiation, and back in the old country I'd be arrested for hooliganism. If you eat a lot of fish, can your body take its own temperature? Think about it.

Thank you, and good night.

The Crybabies of "60 Minutes"

Boy, is Morley Safer ever a sob sister. And that goes double for Mike Wallace and Dan Rather! What's with these guys anyway? Every Sunday night, week after week, it's this guy lost his life savings, that guy sold his arm, and this guy got ripped off by the cheese-of-the-month club. It's enough to make you want to switch to ABC for the Hardy Boys. Now *they're* investigators.

What really gets me is that "60 Minutes" is supposed to be the best investigative-reporting show in the business. This is because Safer, Rather, and Wallace have a lot of flash and look like they're *really* getting to the bottom of things. Morley Safer is considered friendly but tough because he appears . . . friendly but tough. Dan Rather is considered feisty because he appears to be . . . feisty. And Mike "Do you mean to sit there and tell me" Wallace is considered mean because he comes on like he's . . . mean.

But when you get down to it, all they're really doing is crying, weeping, sobbing. Not that I have anything against this particular emotion, but the reporters of "60 Minutes" are always crying over the wrong things. Like the time

Morley Safer uncovered some kind of "diamond scam." It seems they dug up a geezer out on the prairie somewhere within hog-calling distance of Shawnee, Kansas, who spent $12,000 on a telephone diamond deal. In other words, this chump bought some jewels he'd never seen from some jerk he'd never met over the telephone! The diamonds, as it turns out, were worth only $4,000. "I spent a good part of my life savings . . ." this guy tells Morley.

Well boo hoo! You can cry over this poor excuse for an American if you want to, Morley, but I'll tell you what really breaks *me* up about the diamond business! What about all those slaves in Africa who have to haul those diamonds out of the mines? Well, what about them? Do you think they've ever seen $4,000 in their entire lives? Do you think they care about some calcified creep who keeps them in chains by investing in diamonds? As P. T. Barnum said, a sucker is born every 60 minutes. So why don't you just keep your tears to yourself, Morley, unless you can think of something to really cry about?

Then there's Dan Rather. He thinks he stands up to people the way Dry Sack sherry stands up to ice just because he's from Texas. Take the time he went after some really big fish in his incisive exposé "Highway Robbery." This episode found Dan visiting the Georgia Interstate and getting ripped off by crooked gas-station attendants. Can you imagine? Why it's enough to make you . . . well, it's enough to make Dan Rather see red. And not because he's mad! Because he's crying "ain't it a shame!" It seems the "60 Minutes" camera crew got some footage of a long-haired gas jockey in the very act of pouring oil underneath its car to simulate an oil leak. Then, Dan confronted him wearing—what else?—a cowboy hat (presumably something Mike Wallace or Morley Safer could never have done convincingly). "Did you pour oil under my car?" Dan bullied the poor, dumb gas-station attendant, who said no. The following week on "60 Minutes" it was announced that this particular gas station had its franchise license revoked by the oil company (Shell or Gulf or Exxon, I can't remember). But, Dan implied, there are still God-knows-how-many crooked gas-station attendants out there and still God-knows-how-many tourists getting ripped off (sob! sob!), so next time you, with your out-of-state station wagon, go on a cross-country trip, watch out.

A subject more worthy of my tears (and of Rather's bullying) would have been how consumers get ripped off by oil companies, not how some carpetbagger Yankee motorist gets taken for a few bucks by some starving redneck! But no, that wouldn't have provided enough drama. No visuals! Too many sides to the story! "6o Minutes" sticks to the stuff with two—and only two—sides (good guys vs. bad guys) because the Truth supposedly lies approximately due north of center. And it's easier to get people to cry over simpleminded drivel about good and bad. Never mind that the targets are a few big fish in a small barrel. We're supposed to get upset, that's all! Get outraged! Write a letter to "6o Minutes"!

Lest we forget the biggest crybaby of them all, Mike Wallace, one would do well to recall the time he interviewed film director Robert Altman. The reason behind the decision to send Wallace instead of Safer or Rather is obvious: Altman is a Hollywood renegade; he does what he wants, not what the studios want him to do; how does he get away with it? That, at least, is the hype surrounding Altman, and anyone perceived as "getting away with something" in a very big way must inevitably account to Mike Wallace because Mike Wallace "goes for the jugular." But is Robert Altman the Devil? Must he be exposed? Is he doing something wrong?

In the "6o Minutes" cosmology the answer to these questions is an unequivocal yes, for why else would Mike Wallace have so relentlessly interrogated a "renegade" film director? The climax of the interview was when Mike

Wallace raised his eyebrows, smirked and popped what was evidently the big question: "Aren't you wasting a lot of the studio's money?" This is the kind of question that implies that we are supposed to be upset if Altman's movies don't break even; we are supposed to be upset that Altman is "wasting money" (even if it's Hollywood's money); we are supposed to be upset that somebody is getting away with something.

Well, I'm not going to cry about Robert Altman's spending habits! I'm not going to cry about the spending habits of the entertainment industry! You want to know what's a dirty shame? I'll tell you what really gets me! "60 Minutes" really gets me, that's what! Those phony temper tantrums that Shana Kilpatrick and James Alexander—or is it the other way around—always have make me sick! And I'm sick and tired of crying over Palestinians, crying over Israelis, crying over land deals in Florida, crying over penny-ante pyramid schemes! You know what I cry about? I cry about the fact that "60 Minutes" is on the air, that's what! I cry about the state of American television journalism! And I say "60 Minutes," a "news" show out of Caesar's Palace by way of *The Front Page*, has to go. Hello, sweetheart, get me rewrite.

God, Man and Johnny Carson

There exists a certain American ritual more fundamental than voting and more symbolic than July 4th fireworks. Like the most highly evolved of ceremonies, it has many facets, elaborate protocol and sacred icons. It is practiced three times a week in the Burbank, California, tabernacle of the National Broadcasting Corporation, and it goes something like this:

The choir plays the opening hymn, a fast-paced, upbeat, jazzy number with a host of horns. Before the hymn finishes, the altar boy intones the blessing: "H-e-e-e-re's Johnny!" and then leads worshipers in the sacramental chanting of "Hi-yo!" as the Reverend of the Rim-Shot Gag materializes from behind the drapes, dressed in well-tailored three-piece vestments.

A crescendo of holy percussion issues from the choir; the High Priest of TV Humor arrives at his center-stage star. With a Bedouin grovel, altar boy Ed McMahon greets this Cardinal of Late-Night Comedy, who waits for the chant of the "Hi-yo's" to subside. What words will he use, what references will he invoke, from what chapter of the scripture will he quote? The multitudes are silent. He smiles slightly. "Hi. I'm Johnny Carson. The head at the foot of your bed."

For the 4,000th-plus time, the American ritual that is the Johnny Carson monologue has begun. Beyond the "Tonight Show" 's audience assembled in the pews there are 20 million of the faithful gathered in front of their glowing television sets.

After the benediction, Johnny usually begins his comedic liturgy with several vaguely amusing topical references. "How many of you saw that weird item in the news today . . . the one about the company that manufactures *brassieres for cows?* Nobody? Well, let's talk about the weather in California. . . . Boy! Is it wet!"

Or, "Boy! Is it dry!"

Or, "Boy! Is it cold!"

Or, "Gee! It was really beautiful today!"

As every American worth his or her citizenship papers knows, this is a cue for the reverent to shout, for the pious to murmur, for the adoring to praise Johnny from whom all jokes flow:

How wet is it?

How hot is it?

How cold is it?

This part of the monologue is an exercise in responsive reading. In the cult of Johnny Carson, it is a moment when the studio audience surrenders itself to a higher power so it can become One with the joke-telling process. Not a few fans have apparently waited all their lives to commune in this humorous rite, judging from the zeal with which they shout their straight lines. "How nice was it?" one woman wanted to know during the wrong part of the monologue. The poor soul was obviously overcome with religious fervor.

The answers never fail to involve at least one word that is part of the Carson canon, such as "Bigfoot" ("It was so beautiful that Bigfoot was seen on a ski lift waxing his feet!") or "Tidy Bowl man" and "Mrs. Olson" ("It was so wet in Los Angeles today, the Tidy Bowl man had to row Mrs. Olson door to door") or "Evel Knievel" ("The weather in Los Angeles is so beautiful, Evel Knievel switched to a seersucker bat!").

Once finished with the weather Johnny focuses briefly on the international scene, touching many philosophical bases, as a good preacher should. However, his forte has for the last few years been jokes about the American political scene.

"I hear Vice President Mondale opened a King Tut gift shop in the White House to keep busy."

"Bert Lance is in the news again. Lance is negotiating to buy the United States so he can print enough money to pay his loans."

"It hurt the president the most when Amy asked for her allowance in German marks."

"I understand that Hamilton Jordan may leave the White House, team up with Billy Carter and start a punk-rock group."

"Now that Jerry Brown is seeing Linda Ronstadt, I hear that Ed Davis is thinking of shacking up with Kate Smith."

Prior to Watergate, Johnny was not known for his political jokes. When the Watergate scandal escalated, he started doing jokes about Nixon. Shortly after Johnny started doing Nixon jokes, Nixon resigned. While there isn't necessarily any cause and effect here, in certain circles it is believed that since Watergate, Johnny's monologue has become an accurate gauge of the nation's mood. After Bert Lance resigned, the *New York Times* editorialized that the night Johnny started doing jokes about Lance signaled Lance's downfall.

Recently, newsman David Brinkley was a "Tonight Show" guest and mentioned to Johnny that reporters in Washington pay attention to his monologue to see what the public is thinking. Certainly it's impossible to say whether Johnny Carson leads public opinion or merely reflects it, but it cannot be denied that he has become a political bellwether.

The political segment of the Carson liturgy is also an interesting barometer of the public's familiarity with topical issues. Often he takes polls: "How many of you watched the president's speech last night?" "How many of you are familiar with the president's energy plan?" There is usually little response. Not long ago, he told a joke about Benedict Arnold, the understanding of which depended upon the listener's knowledge that Benedict Arnold was a traitor. Nobody laughed.

The fact is that Johnny functions as a kind of shaman through which every political, social and cultural trend passes in a deft blend of one-liners, making us realize when information has entered the popular consciousness. When Johnny and his joke writers decide to joke about, say, King Tut, Yassir Arafat or punk rock, they obviously feel certain that millions of Americans have at least heard of these things. If Johnny regularly jokes about these things over a period of weeks, you *know* that they are in the mainstream.

During the mid-'70s uproar over Earl Butz, for example, Johnny did at least one Earl Butz joke every night for weeks. If you didn't know who Butz was the first time, by the third or fourth time you knew that he was a public official who had committed a faux pas. By the sixth or seventh time the name "Earl Butz" was as well-known a Carson buzzword as "Tidy Bowl man" and an equally effective laugh getter.

Although Johnny's political humor is generally the sharpest part of his monologue, he gets his biggest laughs with one-liners about everyday situations: "Let's find H&R Block and give him our 17 reasons why we don't ever want to see his face again. . . . My doctor, Dr. Mandrake Curvy, has a matching set of Baccarat-crystal specimen jars. . . . The great tax man H&R Goniff works out of a booth at the International House of Pancakes. . . . If you do business while having sex with your wife, it's a tax credit. . . ."

Certain words are sprinkled like holy water throughout the monologue, words that he uses in the weather segment mentioned earlier and other touchstones like "Maalox," "Mr. Whipple," "proctologist," "Dolly Parton," "urinary tract," "Tylenol." These words elicit an automatic laugh because they invoke angst in Johnny's disease-prone, sex-worried, middle-aged devotees. (Neil Simon has pointed out via *The Sunshine Boys* that words with a "k" sound are funny, whereas words without a "k" sound are not funny: "cucumber" is funny; "roast beef" is not.)

Perhaps one of the oldest and best-loved facets of Johnny's monologue is the continual implication that Ed McMahon drinks a lot. Alas, America will never know whether this character trait ascribed to Ed is a fiction created for Johnny's show or a fact of Ed's life, but one thing is certain: it's one of the many signs of the cross Johnny makes on the way to his last joke. Any reference to Ed and booze always gets applause. Johnny will say, "Ed celebrates anything," and then, "Ed drinks to Safeway's meat policy," or, "When the flu virus gets into Ed's bloodstream, it forgets what it's there for!"

I've often wondered if, in 30 or 40 years, the replacement for Johnny will make jokes about his sidekick's drug habit ("You know, Free celebrates anything. . . . He smokes to Safeway's meat policy!").

I have heard viewers, generally those who grew up on "Captain Kangaroo" (note the two "k" sounds), dismiss Johnny because he's so predictable, ridicule him for being so "middle class" (he used to begin the ceremonial wisecracking with a golf swing), call Johnny a relic of the martini generation. They're right.

But obviously they've missed the point. For a proper

tribute one must refer to the liturgy of another American icon, quintessentially American in a completely different sense: the Beach Boys. On their *Love You* album, released in 1977, there's a tune by Brian Wilson called "Johnny Carson." Appropriately, it includes a high-school cheer ("Who's the man that we admire / Johnny Carson is a real live wire") and one verse that, as Johnny would say, "says it all":

> *Ed McMahon comes on and says here's Johnny*
> *Every night at 11:30 he's so funny*
> *Don't you think he's such a natural guy*
> *The way he's kept it up could make you cry.**

* From "Johnny Carson" by Brian Wilson. Reproduced by permission of Brother Publishing. Copyright © 1977.

The Good, The Bad, The Don't-You-Ever-Call-Him Ugly!

"There are two kinds of people in the world," Clint Eastwood once rather cosmically observed. "Those who wear the spurs, and those who don't." It was one of the few lines uttered in those dynamically taciturn spaghetti Westerns for which Eastwood has become so admired.

On screen, the line is punctuated by the world-famous *Eastwood squint,* a singular piece of body language that first came to public attention way back when Clint was the star of television's "Rawhide" and traveling under the antiheroic alias Rowdy Yates. It is a squint that, as far as I'm concerned, need not be accompanied by dialogue, for it tells you right away exactly who is wearing the spurs and who is not.

Eastwood has been squinting his way to the top for about 20 years. From his very first roles in such dues-paying films as "Revenge of the Creature" and "Tarantula," to the Man with No Name, to Dirty Harry, he has warded off the forces of evil with the modern-day equiv-

alent of a string of garlic: bad vibes. People have come to
believe in his roles so much that in 1974, during the San
Francisco Zebra killings, a piece of impassioned graffito
asked: "Dirty Harry, where are you when we need you?"

So, like the author of that query and all other Eastwood
fans, I was heartened when I heard that he would be
drifting the high plains again in *Escape from Alcatraz*.
Alcatraz, apparently, is a place from which Eastwood
may never escape, since an earlier film, *The Enforcer*,
culminated in a shootout on that same, symbolically craggy
rock.

My excitement about a new Eastwood film, however,
was somewhat diminished when a few weeks ago in the
beauty parlor I read that Clint had gotten a face-lift!
Fortunately, Eastwood soon stepped forth with a vehe-
ment denial, and I hope he's leveling with us, for the loss
of Eastwood's lines—and I'm not referring to his speaking
lines—will surely mark a sad day in the history of American cinema. Yet, disturbingly, the recent Eastwood *oeuvre*
indicates that, rather than admiring those deep and craggy
wrinkles in the mirror (and they're just *beginning* to get
good), Clint has been contemplating the plot wrinkles in
his latest movies. As many of his fans have been dismayed
to learn, Clint has recently taken to *speaking* on screen.
This, I feel, has been at the expense of his squint.

Consider his characterization of "Dirty Harry," the self-
contained (some might say repressed) cop who fights
crime by himself, lives by himself, eats by himself, and
stars in movies by himself. To facilitate this solo existence,
Dirty Harry's partners always get killed during the first
third of the film. And presumably, any script writer who
dares to include a character with Eastwood's longevity
(about 90 minutes) also goes down for the count.

But, alas, things are starting to change in Dirty Harry
Land. A couple of Dirty Harry's ago, Eastwood's partner
was (gasp!) a woman. That meant that Dirty Harry had

to (a) talk and (b) fall in love. In order for this to happen, *she* had to live longer than any of Dirty Harry's erstwhile sidekicks. And so, after devoting so many years to showing no emotion whatsoever, Dirty Harry almost becomes human. When she gets killed trying to save him (naturally, *before* they have consummated the relationship), Dirty Harry actually gives a few clues as to his inner feelings, then vows to continue fighting crime singlehandedly—this time, in her memory.

All this with barely a squint at all—which, personally, I find alarming. I'll take good ole Dirty Harry any day, the guy who does things alone and squinting, to the new, humanized Harry who actually tries social intercourse—and appears to *think* about the other kind—minus the meaningful eyelocks.

Are Eastwood's squinting days gone forever? In his last movie, *Every Which Way But Loose*, he had the effrontery to star himself with not only a woman, but a chimpanzee as well. This, one assumes, was an unfortunate attempt to follow Burt Reynolds down the avenue of "comic" studs.

I have two things to say about this movie. First: chimpanzees are *not* funny, except when they accidentally get drunk and go on a rampage. In addition, I don't think any Eastwood film needs *another* member of the cast reminding us of our animal instincts. Second: as for the female co-star, Sondra Locke—Clint can do a lot better.

If Eastwood wants a new image, why can't he just put another serape over his head, a long, thin cigar in his mouth, squint at the camera for three hours and call it *Clint?* It would gross $50 million in the first week, easy. Eastwood, after all, is the No. 1 box-office draw in Italy, Japan, and Ohio. Why, in Iran he's bigger than the ayatollah, and the French have invented a dance called "Le Magnum Force." This is not because Eastwood is a master of foreign tongues—or even his own for that matter. No, it's because of his *squint.*

But, as they say, still waters run deep. Flipping through my mental Rolodex of memorable Eastwood lines, I can't help but recall the stirring "A man's got to know his limitations." Apparently this is not a line Clint has taken to heart, because his limitation happens to be any role requiring more than a dozen cue cards.

So when it comes to lines, Clint, take my advice. Keep drifting those high plains—and stick with the squint. Okay?

Dean Martin Roasts Alexander Solzhenitsyn

10:00 (4) DEAN MARTIN—COMEDY SPECIAL: Nobel Prize winner Alexander Solzhenitsyn takes the verbal punches as he is roasted on the third anniversary of his emigration to the Free World by Dean Martin, Bernard Malamud, Svetlana Alliluyeva, Rudolph Nureyev, Henny Youngman, Charo, Muhammad Ali, Howard Cosell and Sammy Davis, Jr.

DEAN MARTIN (*staggering to podium*): Tonight, ladies and gentlemen and esteemed members of the dais, we are honoring a wonderful human being. He's taken a lot of hard knocks like the rest of us. (*Pauses and surveys guests on dais.*) He's gotten his chops busted at almost every bend in the road. But, as we all know, *nothing has stopped him,* because he is a man endowed with courage . . . and a lifetime supply of Russian vodka. (*Sneers.*) Ladies and gentlemen, for our salute to this unbelievable individual, this human being who is as great a man as he is a writer, I'd like to call on my good friend and terrific human being, *Henny Youngman!*
    HENNY YOUNGMAN (*assumes aggressive stance at podium*): Man walks into a bar and says to the bartender, "Gimme a drink." Bartender says, "Why should I? You're

so drunk your breath gives me a nosebleed." You know, Dean, I bet you could get loaded on Scotch tape! Folks, Dean's been thrown out of so many bars that he wears gray suits so he'll match the sidewalk! But seriously folks, Dean's a wonderful person. And speaking of wonderful people, I'd like to give my regards to Alexander Sells-a-lot-of-novels—I mean, Solzhenitsyn. You know, Al, you're beautiful and I love you. I love your books, too. Folks, there's nothing better than settling down in front of a fire-place with a couple of great Russian novels. They make great logs! And Al, I really admire suffering. My wife will kill me for this but she's taught me a lot about suffering. I mean she's so cold her side of the waterbed's frozen. But all kidding aside, folks, my wife's a beautiful person. And so are you, Al. Even though your books are lousy! Frankly, I can't wait till you're deported! I mean you've got a lot of nerve calling yourself a writer! You think it was bad in the Gulag archipelago? Back in—

DEAN MARTIN: Henny, that was a beautiful and moving statement. Ladies and gentlemen, our next dis-tinguished member of the dais to honor Mr. Solzhenitsyn (*slurs name drunkenly*) is that fabulous Coochie-Coochie Girl, *Charo!* Whew! What a hunk of woman!

CHARO: Hey coochie coochie! Alexander, you are bery cute! Your beard is bery sexy! You like to coochie coochie? I coochie all the time with Cugat! Hey coochie—

DEAN MARTIN: Whew! There's really a lot of woman there! Charo, you better sit down before Mr. Solzhenitsyn has to make a very tough decision. Now, I'd like to turn the podium over to my good friend and heavyweight champion of the world, Muhammad Ali. Muhammad, I see you've taken some time off from the Uncle Ben's rice box to add something to tonight's proceedings.

MUHAMMAD ALI: Roses are red, Russia is blue, 'cause Solzhenitsyn is here, and I am too!

DEAN MARTIN (*motions to waiter for refill*): Muhammad, you break me up. Wasn't that great, folks? Please say yes—I'd like to live a few more years. I think it's time to call on one of our honored guest's fellow country-men, Rudolph Nureyev. Rudy, howzabout it?

RUDOLPH NUREYEV (*assumes first position at po-dium*): Thank you very much, Dean. You're a beautiful person. Aren't I a beautiful person? And don't I have a beautiful body? (*Walks in front of podium, executes a flawless grand plié.*) Alexander, if you want to meet some beautiful women, just let me know. Jackie, Lee, Bianca, I know them all. Or if you want to meet some beautiful men, I can arrange that too. I'll even introduce you to Truman Capote if you like. Do not fear, comrade—you will not get arrested for hooliganism like at home. You can do anything you want in the West. Isn't it a wonderful place?

DEAN MARTIN: Now, that's what I call a right-on testimonial to freedom! Rudy, you're a wonderful human being and it's been a real privilege for the Free World to get to know you. And speaking of privileges and the Free World, it is my privilege to introduce Svetlana Alliluyeva, who proves without a doubt how great it is to be an American!

SVETLANA ALLILUYEVA: Mr. Solzhenitsyn, if my father were here today, you would not be very popular. Nobody would read your books. They would read only mine—

DEAN MARTIN: She's only kidding, folks. Right, Svetlana? What a sense of humor those Russians have! I bet her father was a real card. I think it's time to hear from the most beloved member of the dais, Howard Cosell.

HOWARD COSELL: Dean, you're cute. Real cute. Folks, I wouldn't say that Dean Martin has a drinking problem, but if a mosquito bit him, it would die of alcohol poisoning. (*Laughs.*) But we're not here to talk about

Dean Martin. We're here to pay homage to Alexander Solzhenitsyn. The greatest writer of our time. Mr. Big. Mr. Brains. Mr. Typewriter. And, if I may paraphrase myself, the Killer from Siberia. He's taken guff from no one. He's a real champ. Even Ali couldn't K.O. the likes of the Soviet Politburo. I'd like to thank you, Mr. Solzhenitsyn, for many thrilling moments in the fast-moving and action-packed world of sports—I mean literature. You've really got the crowd on your side. And if you'd like to go a few rounds with Mailer, let me be the first to know.

DEAN MARTIN: Thanks, Howard. That was about as stimulating as a mouthful of sawdust and water. Which paves the way for a tribute from the well-known man of letters, Bernard Malamud. Say, Bernie, didn't I see you the other night with a good-lookin' blonde?

BERNARD MALAMUD (*with stern expression on his face*): I don't think it's necessary to make remarks like that, Mr. Martin. This is a very solemn occasion. I mean it isn't every day that a chronicler of oppression such as myself gets to meet another such writer whose works have depressed and saddened even more readers! Alex—you don't mind if I call you that, do you?—you have profoundly influenced me. Especially the way you describe prison gruel—

DEAN MARTIN (*sipping from martini glass*): Very poignant, Bernie. It's been an honor to hear from you. And now, ladies and gentlemen, I'd like to introduce Golda Meir's favorite entertainer, Sammy Davis, Jr.

SAMMY DAVIS, JR.: Too much, Dean. Like too much. You really break me up . . . *pizza face.* Folks, I kid Dean. Like, I really love him. My wife and I had him over to the pad the other day and it was really beautiful. We rapped about a lot of things. Like why we love this country. We love this country because it has been so good to us. I mean where else could a black man such as myself become a

Jew and still get to hang out with Peter Lawford? But
seriously, folks, there is nothing more moving than the
sight of Alexander Solzhenitsyn on this dais. Because this
dais sits on *free soil,* man. Think about it. It's too groovy
for words. Al, I know this sounds crazy, but I feel like I'm
your brother. Your *soul brother.* Can you dig it? Like, I'm
a Jew, man, and there are a lot of Jewish cats in Russia
who are in a lot of trouble. And I know you left because
of *them.* Al, my man, I know where you're coming from
and I can really get behind it. Like, I've just got to *hug
you,* man—

DEAN MARTIN (*hurriedly staggering to podium*):
Sammy, thank you from the bottom of my heart. You are
truly a beautiful human being. Well, I guess that about
wraps it up, folks. I'd like to congratulate our honored
guest, Alexander Solzhenitsyn (*slurs name*), and offer our
heartfelt—

JERRY LEWIS (*runs up to podium from wings, grabs
microphone*): Dean, excuse me. Ladies and gentlemen, all
of you know that Dean and I aren't exactly on speaking
terms, but I just had to be here. I mean this occasion is so
beautiful and I felt that God wanted me to be here for
this blessed and wonderful event I mean I just had to meet
this marvelous human being I'll just be here a minute
Dean I just gotta ask Al one question so let me just say
how humbled I am to be in the presence of this *modern
saint,* this remarkable human being who has done more
for America than anybody, even more than the President,
this truly amazing little man who stood up to those *shmoes*
in Russia I cry whenever I think about it Dean I've just
gotta ask him *one question* so just give me another minute of your time, ladies and gentlemen. IS THAT TOO
MUCH TO ASK, FOLKS? Al, if you say yes to this question I'll be the luckiest guy in the whole world. I'll know
that my life has been *full of meaning!* I'll know that I

have followed the *right path*! I'll know that my fans in France haven't been wrong! PLEASE SAY YES! Al, would you appear next year on my Muscular Dystrophy Telethon?

THIS BIG

WORLD

OF OURS

Ohio: It's Between Indiana and Pennsylvania

Ohio is known to Ohioans as the Buckeye State. Upon entering Ohio you see signs that say "Welcome to Ohio, the Buckeye State." Upon leaving Ohio you see signs that say "We hope you enjoyed your stay in Ohio, the Buckeye State." I grew up in Ohio and used to wonder what that label connoted to out-of-staters.

According to a friend who was born and raised in Florida (the Sunshine State), Buckeye State is the name of a hotel she once stayed at in Zanesville (home of Zane Grey). A native of Michigan (Land of Lakes) confesses to having "no idea" as to the significance of Buckeye State. And, I must also report, neither do I. The dictionary says the buckeye is "a North American tree with upright flower clusters and glossy brown nuts." Buckeye, it says, can also refer to the nut of this tree. Well, I learned *that* in school; still, I don't know what the buckeye looks like, if it is hard on the outside and soft on the inside, if it tastes sweet or sour or even if it is edible.

The fact that nearly every other state in the Union has a license-tag label that allows you to instantly picture what the state has to offer is probably the first thing that gives Ohioans a feeling of being, well, indescribably different. Not only does the buckeye seem elusive and weird, it provides the native with absolutely no clue to his or her character. If you were born in Missouri and have an I.Q. of 43, you are still able to go through life secure in the knowledge that your state exhorts others to "Show Me"—the implication being that Missourians are basically skeptics.

A ready-made identity is a nice thing for a state to provide, especially if it has as much cachet as "Show Me," "Land of Enchantment" (New Mexico) or "Little Rhody" (guess what state that is). Ohioans are basically buckeyes—whatever that is. They identify with no singular geography, no interesting character trait, not even any particularly exciting historical moment (except for the time Congressman Wayne Hays admitted he was having an affair with Elizabeth Ray). Taught from an early age that Ohio is first in cash registers, coffins, playing cards, Bibles, racing sulkies, rubber, and Liederkranz cheese, the young Ohioan is plagued with regional confusion. Add the crowning piece of bewilderment—"Son, you're a buckeye and don't you forget it"—and you've created (A) interesting people who are forced to forge their own identities—and, having done that, gleefully thumb their noses at the rest of the nation; or (B) thousands of slightly dazed dullards.

Let us first dispense with Group B. Basically, Group B resides in Dayton, Ohio, the city where most of the nation's product testing is done. Daytonians are the people who allow representatives of Hellmann's mayonnaise or Janitor-in-a-Drum to invade their households on the pretense of market research. Have you ever noticed all of the housewives from Dayton who appear in television commercials endorsing this particular microwave oven or that particular vacuum cleaner? (Incidentally, Phil Donahue, the housewife's pal on the national Donahue show, is a Daytonian.)

Some might argue that Dayton must be receiving something in exchange for this invasion of privacy, but judging from the fact that it has been deemed perpetually "average," I don't think it's receiving anything but free cases of Turtle Wax. If anyone with half a brain lived in Dayton, they'd send the Madison Avenue canvassers to Terre Haute, Indiana, for some really average housewives. But no—these people would rather spend their brief moment here on earth testing new improved Boraxo! Still, there is an irony. For all the bafflement and anonymity of the buckeyes in Dayton, *they're* the people who inflict their taste on the rest of the country. If they don't like the new Kool-Aid flavor, you'll probably never get a chance to taste it for yourself. Think about that!

Which brings us to Group A, interesting people who have forged their own identities—either by necessity or lack of anything better to do. These are the natives who generally do not live in Ohio, who have gone on to seek fame and fortune elsewhere, Ohioans being for the most part too stymied to appreciate their talent until they see that it is accepted by the rest of the States. Now, before you say, "Hey, that's the way it is in any small town," let's remember that Ohio is not a small town. Like any area bordered by a lake and a river, it is diverse: it has large department stores, steel mills, millionaires, paupers, athletes and farmers (one of whom once said of the Ohio soil that it "needed only to be tickled with the hoe to laugh with the harvest"—and has since gone on to write for *Grit* magazine). Although Easterners consider Ohio the "Midwest," possibly because of Big Ten football, it is basically in New York City's sphere of influence, being closer to Manhattan than to Chicago or Milwaukee. Essentially, Ohio is a state of mind.

That is a description formulated by my friend Susan Toepfer, born and raised in Cincinnati, now an editor at the New York *Daily News*. Susan eschews regular visits to the homeland but feels there is something about it that provides natives with an unusual sense of security (if not humor). "Because there is a lack of sophistication in Ohio," she explains, "Ohioans are concerned not with style but substance. In New York or Los Angeles, you always hear people say, 'Now look, I'm going to be really honest with you.' This is not a line you hear in Ohio because the idea that you shouldn't be honest never occurs. This is the kind of consciousness that produces more basic truths than, say, California consciousness."

And why isn't Kansas or Nebraska a state of mind? Consider the fact that Ohio has produced more comedians and humorists than any other state. There's Bob Hope, Dean Martin, Jonathan Winters, Phyllis Diller, Paul Lynde, Danny Thomas, Martin Mull, James Thurber, Billy Saluga, Fred Willard, Don ("Father Guido Sarducci") Novello, several National Lampoon writers and, no doubt, a diaspora of equally funny but lesser known jokesters. Ohio has also produced certain "types" in acting: Paul Newman, Doris Day, Roy Rogers, Hopalong Cassidy, Burgess Meredith and Clark Cable. Ohio is known as the "Mother of Presidents"—elementary-school students sing a song that goes "Ohio where the residents keep right on growing presidents"; this refers to William Henry Harrison, U. S. Grant, Rutherford B. Hayes, James A. Garfield, Benjamin Harrison, William McKinley, William Howard Taft and Warren G. Harding (whose Teapot Dome scandal was possibly more notorious than Nixon's Watergate).

Significantly, the state that brought us Warren G. Harding, the country's first punk president, has also brought us the best originators of punk rock: Devo (Akron), the Dead Boys (Cleveland) and Pere Ubu (Cleveland). Considering the influence these personalities and phenomena have had on the country, it would seem that Ohio has a lot to do with what everybody is laughing at, dancing to and voting for. (Ohio, in fact, is considered a pivotal state

in the voting of the electoral college; any presidential candidate who loses Ohio will probably lose the election.)
So, you might be wondering, what's the big idea? What is
there in the personality of the displaced buckeye that
compels him or her to tell the rest of the country what to
do and what to laugh at? Perhaps further dissection of
the buckeye personality is called for.

When meeting a buckeye outside his or her natural hab-
itat, you've probably noticed that he or she will giggle,
shuffle or joke defensively when faced with the question
"Where are you from?" Oregonians, Texans or Pennsyl-
vanians do not, in my experience, seem to be as embar-
rassed as Ohioans when discussing point of origin. This
can only be attributed to a long legacy of rather silly ac-
complishments associated with the state.

You can count on anyone hailing from *Cleveland,* for
example—a national joke word in itself—to grin sheepishly
and describe that city with an unusual form of civic pride
as the "Mistake on the Lake." Cleveland, a site of sup-
purating industrial wealth, is located on the mouth of the
once-pristine Cuyahoga River (that means "winding" to
you palefaces), which several years ago also became a
national joke word because it caught fire. Now that we're
on the subject, former Mayor Ralph J. Perk achieved national prominence, not for his expertise as an administra-
tor, but for his lack of it when wielding—of all things—
a blowtorch, at the christening of a building. He set his
hair on fire. Later, Perk again splashed big when his wife
turned down an invitation to the White House because it
interfered with her bowling night. Bowling is no joke in
Cleveland; in fact, many of my high-school classmates
aspired to the exalted position of pin setter at the Kingpin
Bowling Alley. Perhaps the most telling Cleveland story
is the one about the two teens who paid a friend $60 to
kill their father. Now, $60 may not sound like much to
you, but in a town where poor kids grow up to be either

golf caddies or deluded minions of the jukebox racket, it
has a certain ring to it. Hence, the pubescent assassin got
his man. Then the children reportedly left Dad's body lying in their home for ten days while they went on a shopping spree with his cash and credit cards. "He wouldn't
let us do anything we wanted," they later told police, "like
smoke pot."

Judging from the frequency with which Cincinnati is
used in punch lines, it is second in comedic value only to
Cleveland. Natives of Cincinnati are known to chuckle
disparagingly when they are forced to repeat the Chamber
of Commerce slogan for that once-sparkling gem of the
Ohio River: the "Queen City." This is actually a variation
on the phrase "Queen of the West," a description of Cincinnati penned by Henry Wadsworth Longfellow long before Cincinnati came to be characterized by breweries,
Astroturf, Fleischmann's yeast and Procter and Gamble
(known locally as Procter and God). A clue to the disdain
displaced Cincinnatians have for their hometown can be
found in the delightfully euphemistic travel-book description of it as "no laggard culturally." One recent example
of local culture is the Flat Earth Society, which advertises
in the classified sections of national magazines. It exhorts
readers to "join and regress."

And then, of course, there's Columbus, state capital. In
other words, this is whence Governor James "Kent State"
Rhodes rules. It is also headquarters of Larry Flynt and
the country's first Sopor factory. About the former, we
need say nothing, except that Flynt has a replica of the
Kentucky shack where he grew up in the basement of his
Columbus mansion. About the latter, we are baffled. Why
aren't the locals more excited about the fact that Columbus was the city that first told the rest of the country to go
to sleep? Although Sopors are no longer produced in Columbus and are no longer called Sopors (a derivative of
"soporific"—so much richer than Quaalude!), downers

have certainly assumed their place in the country's medi-
cine cabinet—and that's another significant Ohio fact!

Not to be outdone in civic pride are natives of many
other Ohio towns. "Even if I have my head up my ass,"
observes a relocated buckeye, "it smells better than Youngstown." A native of Sandusky points rather reluctantly to
the big news that Charles Dickens once ate at a local restaurant called the Porter House. He reportedly liked the
steaks so much that he told all his friends about it—
thereby contributing the phrase "porterhouse steak" to the
national lexicon. "Answer this!" demands a Chillicothe native. "How come if there's over 90 colleges in Ohio, everybody's so stupid?" Possibly, this man was referring, among
other things, to Xenia, Ohio, a town whose plucky population is annually depleted by the same killer tornado.

To grasp the complexities of these regional riddles, your
reporter, a self-proclaimed member of Group A (having
joined the exodus thereof at an early age), has conducted
revealing interviews with several well-known buckeyes
(one of whom wonders why other states do not, like Ohio,
have a "state nut").

"I think just as many pharmacists as comedians come
from Ohio," reports Martin Mull, "but you never hear
about them." Mull was first seen nationally on "Mary Hartman, Mary Hartman" (which took place in the mythical
town of Fernwood, Ohio). Ohio was chosen as the site for
the show, he says, because "it was less work for the type-
setters." He lived in Ohio for 14 years, first in North Ridge-
ville, then in North Olmstead—both suburbs of Cleveland.
Mull, apparently, does not seem to have been absent the
day his class made the field trip to the nearest buckeye
grove. "A buckeye is a nut that falls off trees, isn't it?" he
says. "Either that or a sticker that Woody Hayes puts on
helmets when his men do well."

Mull's "America 2-Night" sidekick, Fred Willard, is also
from Ohio. "I spent the first sixteen years of my life in

Cleveland," he says, "and if someone had asked me if I wanted to leave when I was twelve, I would have said yes." Willard feels that the reason so many comedians come from Ohio is that "you have to laugh at yourself for being there. Ohio is not one way or the other, not north or south, it's just there. Even *it* doesn't know what it is—the license plates don't even say 'The Buckeye State.' They say 'Fasten your seat belts.'" Like any wily Ohioan, Willard knows that a buckeye is anyone from Ohio but was surprised to learn that the buckeye is, in fact, a nut.

"I saw a little brown nut," states Jerry Rubin, a Cincinnati native, when describing a buckeye. "I'm not sure though. Is that what it is? I'm not patriotic about Ohio." Also placing high in this category is Billy Saluga, a Youngstown native and former member of the Ace Trucking Company. Recently, he has become noted for his "You can call me Ray Jay" routine. "I don't know what a buckeye is," he admits. "It's a kind of nut, isn't it?"

Phyllis Diller grew up in Lima, Ohio. She says she was born in a manger. She left Ohio "when the crops failed" and figures there are so many comedians and presidents from Ohio because "the school system there was great in the old days." A buckeye is "a nut," she says definitively.

Earl Wilson, the syndicated columnist noted for his "pearls," is from the town of Rockport, Ohio. "A buckeye is a form of nut from a tree," reports Earl. "I used to carry 'em around. It's a round-looking object as big as a couple of marbles." (Mull describes the buckeye as resembling a "baby's butt.") Wilson left Ohio because he was a newspaperman and wanted to get to New York. "All middle-west newspapermen wanted to get to New York," he says. "There's a story they used to tell about coming from Ohio. This was at a gathering somewhere in Massachusetts. A woman asked an Ohio woman, 'Where do you come from?' The Ohio woman said, 'I come from Ohio.' The Massachusetts woman said, 'That's funny. Where I come from, we pronounce it I-o-way.' " Earl believes that the "middle-western approach to life" accounts for the abundance of comedians from Ohio. "They're hayseeds, I guess. It's the hayseeds' approach to life." He delights in retelling a James Thurber story about Ohioans. Thurber got to New York, the story goes, and he found a cocktail party where all the people from Ohio were standing off in one corner. They were all saying what a great place Ohio was. One jealous Texan walked over and said, "If Ohio's so great, why didn't you stay there?" An Ohioan replied, "Out there, competition was too tough."

As for outright regional chauvinism, the only person willing to admit fondness for the state was Billy Saluga. "Youngstown is a shitty town," he says, "but I had a nice life there. I go back every now and then. The people are really lovely. Of course maybe that's because I'm well known. I always liked it, though." Jerry Rubin, who left Ohio when he was 21, says he "didn't know enough to leave sooner. Everything I did was a rebellion against Cincinnati. The people there felt they knew everything. I don't think there's anything special about Ohio. Maybe Michigan."

There is an old riddle about Ohio which buckeyes have gotten as much mileage out of as Firestone (headquarters: Akron) has out of its radial tires. It was recently set to a punk beat in the song "Jocko Homo" by Devo and perhaps is the last word on the Buckeye State:

> *I gotta rhyme*
> *That comes in a riddle*
> *O-HI-O*
> *What's round on the ends*
> *High in the middle*
> *O-HI-O*

Ohio Fact Roundup

Area: 41,222 square miles

Population: 10,652,017

Capital: Columbus

What to do in Columbus:
See Colo, the world's first
captive-born gorilla

Largest city: Cleveland

What to do in Cleveland:
Eat pistachios in the lobby
of the Terminal Tower.

Highest point: Campbell
Hill, 1,550 feet

Lowest point: Birthplace of
George Steinbrenner

Hippest point: Alan Freed's
apartment

Settled in: 1788

Admitted to Union: March 1,
1803

Popular name: Buckeye State

State flower: Scarlet carna-
tion

State beverage: Carling
Black Label Beer

State bird: Locust

Getting there: Greyhound
and Trailways buses have
been known to disappear
into the mysterious "Ohio
Triangle"; safer to be a
native and take a bus *out*

Festivals: Maple, Cherry
Blossom, Big Bend
Regatta, Swiss Cheese,
Pottery, Soap-Box Derby,
Parade of the Hills, Sweet
Corn, Tool and Die,
International Mining and
Manufacturing, Pumpkin,
Apple Butter, National
Clay Week

Jamborees: Grape

Trailer parks: Lazy Acres,
Geneva; Roundup Lake
Park, Mantua; Blue Heron
Service Plaza, Ohio Turn-
pike, exit 12

Historic sites: Fallen Timbers
Park, on U.S. 24 south-
west of Maumee, where
General "Mad Anthony"
Wayne defeated the In-
dians and Chief Turkey
Foot in 1794; Serpent
Mound, four miles north-
west of Locust Grove off
State 73, largest effigy In-
dian mound in America;
John Glenn Bathtub,

Official form of entertainment: High-school reunions

Motto: "With God, All Things Are Possible—including a record contract for Pure Prairie League"

Farm receipts: $2 billion

Formerly wealthy suburb from which white people have recently fled: Shaker Heights

Minerals: What's left is at the Gem Club in Toledo

Morality: John Dean

Shopping malls: Ranks third in nation

Rock bands that started at shopping malls: James Gang, Outsiders

Immigrants: See Cleveland's West Side and Ohio River's "Ruhr Valley" section

Most Memorable Pilot: Thurmon Munson

where the astronaut slipped and hurt his head, in suburban Cleveland home

Industrial tours: Recycled Pantyhose Industrials, Akron; Whirlpool Corporation, Clyde; National Cash Register Company, Dayton; Eastman Kodak Company, Findlay; Procter and Gamble, Ivorydale; Slagco Steel Unlimited, Middletown; J.M. Smucker Company, Orrville; Scott Paper Company, Sandusky; The Blade and Toledo Times, Toledo; Velvet Ice Cream Company, Utica; Kishman Fish Company, Vermilion

Useful phrases: "Chateaubriand for two." "Dennis Kucinich is a maniac." "Governor Rhodes knows what he's doing." "Excuse me, I have to go iron my dress shields."

Summer Camps as Advertised in the Special-Interest Section of "The New York Times Magazine"

SUMMER IN BEIRUT. For culture vultures only! Learn about another culture while living in a PLO home. Tours, sightseeing, sports, social activities, theater. 12th great season! Also: Pony Trek Through the South Bronx and White Water Rafting Down Love Canal. Write to Unusual Adventures, P.O. Box 18, Portland, Ore.

THERAPY-IN-THE-PINES. An interdenominational retreat for nonsectarian executive women. If you're like most overachieving businesswomen, you're probably suffering from a severe neurosis that prevents you from achieving even more. The staff of this unique therapeutic environment knows that whenever you've tried to get in touch with your feelings, the line is always busy. After spending just two weeks in this amazingly supportive haven located in the famous forests of Rhodachusetts, you'll feel that you deserved that salary raise—and will be ready to ask for another one! "Where Growth Is More Than a Noun." Dr. Martha Rehnquist-Blocking, 75 Columbus Avenue, Upper West Side, New York City, N.Y.

PUBLISHING FARM. Create a lasting piece of gay literature while learning the fascinating rudiments of running a farm. We offer a wide range of living arrangements depending on your budget. For those with one or two unpublished novels under their Adolfo belts, there is the simple yet charming Quentin Crisp Bunk, whereas for those who have published at least one self-consciously witty rhyme in a small-press poetry anthology, we provide the somewhat more lavish Oscar Wilde Cabin. The final day of the season features a reading of completed manuscripts before selected representatives of the William Morris Agency, and a demonstration of tractor skills. "Bring Your Own Wite-out." Write: Two Guys with a Concept, Turnpike Exit Ramp 91, Jefferson City, Mo.

OUTWARD-BOUND FACIALS. Test your survival skills in the untamed waterways and coastal islands of Maine. From camp base on scenic Penobscot Bay, we drop you at an uninhabited wilderness site, where your assignment is to live for two months and come back well groomed. Tweezers from a clam shell, moisturizer from sea kelp, a bath with a real live sponge—imagine how much you'll love this unusual cosmetic odyssey! Write for further details to Dave, Box 296, Cheap Vacations, Me.

CAMP HOLE-IN-ONE. Arnold Palmer may be a master of the green, but "the other Arnold" Pinkney is the duke

of Astroturf—and we have him! Now you can brush up
your putting by spending a summer of intensive study
with the world-renowned miniature-golf authority in a
carefully controlled miniature-golf environment. Campers
are offered the unique opportunity to specialize in one
particular golf style by selecting a theme course on which
to spend their entire summer. Choose from Dutch Farm
Country, the Everglades, or Prehistoric Times. Write:
Camps with Names That Sound Vaguely Indian, P.O. Box
99, Grand Central Station, New York City, N.Y.

TAWDRY MANOR.   Seductively poised on the simmer-
ing delta near the half-parted mouth of the Pulsating
River, this languid antebellum plantation urges you to
spend a sultry summer behind its mysteriously half-closed
doors. Write: Torrid Trips, Throbbing Acres, La.

GARNI ON A SHOESTRING.   Spend an inexpensive
culinary summer specializing in the preparation of cute
food such as marinated zucchini with dill, smoked mozzarella and tomato with basil, and yogurt-dipped new po-
tatoes with Jason. Located on Florida's inspiring Omelet
Key. Write to Fat Homosexual Chefs, 1200 Carbo Boulevard, Baltimore, Md.

CAMP SOCIAL.   Is "party" your middle name? Do you
live to "boogie"? "Boogie" to live? If you answered yes to
all three questions, consider this an invitation to a 90-day
party high atop fabulous Mt. Mouton Cadet deep inside
Canada's fabulous province of Quebec. Camp Social, a
subsidiary of the nationwide chain of Fun Clubs (all
rights reserved), features an indoor disco, outdoor disco,
disco rec room, disco color war, and disco canoe trips
(during which you will perfect those all-important disco
portage skills). The summer-long fun fest climaxes in an
adventure trek to Popper Hollow, at which point even

more excitement ensues as campers consume quantities of amyl nitrite and simultaneously rappel down a treacherous cliff on their way back to Camp Social! R.S.V.P.: through your local Fun Club.

CLOSET LAKE. Special facility for asthmatic conservatives. A beautiful desert oasis in the healthful saguaro region of southwestern Arizona, this unique camp has provided an atmosphere of rest, relaxation, and Robitussin for wheezing Republicans. Activities limited to making public statements disavowing homosexual tendencies, and breathing. Special discount for congressmen. Write to Untraceable Mail Drop, Reno, Nev.

HISTORY CAMP. Finally, a summer retreat exclusively for history buffs. Offers "The Story of America" in two-, four-, or six-week sessions. Six-day session includes in-depth analysis of European influences. Also featuring field trips to historians' homes, and at end of each session, a surprise visit from an important historical figure. "A Camp with a Purpose." Send your query to Paul Revere, Ulysses S. Grant Way, Harriet Tubman Village, Ohio.

JOAN CRAWFORD RANCH. Seventy-five years of theatrical tradition and innovative camping concepts provide a unique experience in living and learning. Each season features a rigorous program of instruction in such important areas as lipstick application, personal poise, and child abuse. The session culminates in our annual production of *Mildred Pierce,* aided by a talented trio of aging drama coaches who claim to have known Joan Crawford. Pre-prepared letters home with clever "Mommie Dearest" salutation. "It's Camp!" For information write the Joan Crawford Estate, Box 5000, Hollywood, Calif.

Coping with Reagan

Remedial Activism for the Ronald Reagan Years: A Multimedia Experience, Part I. A refresher course in protest taught by demonstration expert Bruce Marcus, a veteran of many confrontations, including Selma, People's Park, Days of Rage, and the levitation of the Pentagon.

—From the catalogue for
the Modern School for
Adult Education at Night

It was a big night for lectures. There was a line five blocks long for the seminar on cooking with a wok. Hundreds of people were waiting for the slide show on travel in the Caribbean. Werner Fassbinder arrived for the "round table" on film, and three people were trampled in the stampede for admission.

But the biggest crowd of all waited for Bruce Marcus, Ph.D., in the sociobiology of protest. The strains of Bob Dylan singing "All Along the Watchtower" filled the hall, and Dr. Marcus marched purposefully to the lectern. The veteran activist sported a short beard and moustache, and a historic button that said, "Majority for a silent Agnew." He had the demeanor of a prankish scholar.

"Hey, when was the last time any of you were on the receiving end of a tear-gas canister?" Dr. Marcus began. There was a barrage of answers.

"With the Yippies in Miami."

"Don't you mean the Zippies?"

"SDS in Albuquerque."

"Moratorium in Bryant Park."

"Impeach Nixon at DuPont Circle."

"A prison riot at Folsom."

Dr. Marcus chuckled knowingly. "Well," he said, "new times call for new types of action. Political protest should fit the temper of the time. A tactic that in the 1960s may have resulted in 435 column inches of coverage and the first ten minutes of all three network news shows, on the same day, may today net an entire media blackout—thus rendering the activity a complete waste of time. Any questions so far?"

"What should I wear to a rally against U.S. involvement in El Salvador?" a woman in the front row called out.

"Oh, we'll get to that," said Dr. Marcus as he headed for the blackboard. "But first let's see what there is to protest during the Reagan years. After all, there's no war yet, so what else is there?"

"Food stamp cutbacks!" several people called out in unison.

"Of course, of course," Dr. Marcus said. "But that's obvious. What about the entire Bill of Rights?" he demanded, scrawling in chalk. "And then there's Republican policy on pet adoption centers, Republican policy on Granada, Republicans who use tax dollars to visit Granada, Republican policy on . . . I think you're beginning to get the picture."

"What about Reagan's family?" a young man asked. "They're pretty weird."

"Weird?" Dr. Marcus replied. "The Reagan family gives new meaning to the term *weird*. I think that the president's son is vulnerable on the grounds that tax dollars should not be used to protect ballet dancers."

"There must be more to get mad about than that," shouted an aspiring protestor in a blue leotard.

"You bet," said Dr. Marcus, returning to the blackboard and hurriedly adding to his list. "I think we can expect the disappearance of funding for institutions that make things that come out of a kiln."

"I don't see what's wrong with that," said a smartly dressed woman. "All it means is that next time I have a dinner party, I can serve food on dishes that are all the same size."

"Maybe you have a point," Dr. Marcus said, and then added: "Well, I still think you can expect the reappearance of prayer in school, the Krugerrand, Nancy Kissinger, Mitch Miller sing-alongs, and men who wear hats whenever they go out."

The professor then scurried over to a record player, plunked down an album, and turned it on. "One, two, three, four, we don't want your fucking war!" It was the sound of half a million people, surging through the streets of Washington, D.C., chanting against the Vietnam War. "This sonorous chant," Dr. Marcus said, "could easily become 'One, two, three, four, Ronnie is a fucking bore!'"

"How about 'One, two, three, four, George Bush makes me sore!'" a young man called out.

"Cute," Dr. Marcus agreed, "but there may be some confusion as to whether you mean 'sore' as in angry, or 'soar' as in fly." Then the record player blared "Big firms get rich, G.I.'s die!" "Versatile, isn't it?" Dr. Marcus asked. "It easily withstands the test of time and can fit nearly any unpopular involvement."

Suddenly the lights went off, a screen was lowered, and slides began to flash on and off. An hors d'oeuvre–fed model from the pages of *Elle* magazine appeared. "Now for one of the most popular topics," Dr. Marcus smiled. "What to wear to a demonstration. Note the pith helmet," he said, outlining it with a pointer. "And the army fatigues. This means that the uniform of the activist is now an accepted style of the day. In fact, I noted that some of you are actually dressed for a demonstration. Why don't you go out and start one?"

Three people in jumpsuits immediately filed out of the hall. The lights flashed on.

"What about Spandex?" a new-waver inquired.

"I've heard it absorbs mace," Dr. Marcus said, "although I haven't seen any research. Also, no one has yet developed a tear-gas-proof mascara, and, according to my wife, this can be quite unpleasant. One final fashion tip— do not wear coke spoons to a mass rally. I've heard that the Reagan regime is planning to outlaw tiny silverware. There is even speculation," Dr. Marcus warned, "that its transportation across interstate lines may constitute grounds for a conspiracy indictment."

"How can you tell who's a cop these days?" wondered a veteran of many demonstrations. "Everyone looks hip."

"It's a problem," Dr. Marcus acknowledged. "The cop used to be the guy with the longest hair, loudest mouth, and strawberry rolling papers." He unfurled a full-length chart with a picture of the quintessential male and female hippie. "Or it was the woman in the miniskirt and Nehru jacket who did not realize," he explained, pointing to her legs, "that she wasn't supposed to shave."

The cunning Dr. Marcus offered a useful tip. "Remember in World War II movies when G.I. Joe asked the Nazi provocateur who won the 1932 World Series? Well, today's anti-Reaganite might want to ask a suspected cop to name, for example, the Chicago Eight." Then he erased the blackboard and began to scribble quickly. "Please make note of the following spy-detecting questions: Did you get firehosed in Selma? Who is William Kunstler? How much is an ounce of Humboldt County sinsemilla selling for these days?"

"What if the cop knows the answers?" someone shouted. "What if there's a bust?"

"Always be prepared for a bust," Dr. Marcus stated

solemnly. "Years ago you probably used to write the ACLU phone number on your wrist before attending a demonstration. Today, things are different. The number you should wear on your wrist, in case of a bust, is your agent's."

"You mentioned media response to a demonstration," a man in a Mao cap said. "How do we get that?"

"That's a good one," Dr. Marcus chuckled. "When it comes to antiestablishment activism, the press generally adopts a tone somewhere between that of a prison warden and a substitute teacher: 'Sure, there are a lot of things wrong with the system, but do you have any better ideas?' Basically, the press feels it was used in the sixties. To quote the Who, reporters seem to have vowed not to get fooled again. In other words, expect questions designed to elicit replies that have nothing to do with your demonstration. For instance, if there is a nationwide rally in front of every capital building in every state because Reagan has just announced a blockade of Cuba, the press will undoubtedly ignore the issue and ask such incisive questions as 'Isn't this reminiscent of the sixties?' 'Didn't this go out with love beads?' and 'Couldn't you make your point more successfully by writing your congressmen?' "

"So what are we supposed to say?" the man in the Mao cap wanted to know.

"Here's a reply that can be used to field any ill-conceived query," Dr. Marcus said, picking up a stack of mimeographed sheets. "Take one and pass it back." The sheet said:

> The reason we're here, Bob/Michelle, is to point out that Cuba has nothing to do with the insurgents on St. Bart's, and blockading the island is something Jack Lord would do on "Hawaiian Eye."

"This reply," said Dr. Marcus, "effectively sidesteps any verbal minefield set by the press, explains why the demonstration has been called, and makes an all-important television reference, which, of course, anyone viewing the interview will understand. Questions, comments, criticism?"

"Is it okay for a woman to ask a man to go to a demonstration?" a woman responded.

"Are you asking?" Dr. Marcus joked. "Actually, I was afraid someone would bring that up. The social protocol of protest is tricky. Many of you are probably wondering when to exchange phone numbers—before or after the bust? And what if you attend a demonstration with a date, and run into partners from a previous protest? These problems plague even the most seasoned activist," Dr. Marcus admitted. "In my experience, there are several things men and women should never say to each other when on the barricades. Please make note.

"Guys, never approach a prospective picketing pal with 'Hey, I'm a feminist, too,' 'I was almost raped once myself,' or 'I can't believe some of the lines men use just to get a cup of sankaccino.'

"On the other hand, gals, it seems that you can approach a chanting chum and say just about anything, provided it's not something like 'Was John the eggman or the walrus? I always forget.'"

"Are there any effective demonstration ice-breakers?" one man wanted to know.

"Well," thought Dr. Marcus, "there are suitable opening lines for either men or women. Among conscientious activists, such as Single Parents for the Separation of Church and State, there is the provocative 'If you don't vote, have you abdicated your responsibility as a citizen?' Among hedonistic activists, such as Single Parents for Sex Education in Public Schools, there is the romantic 'Let's get naked and smoke.' And for lonely activists, such as Underground Singles Against the Draft, there is the furtive 'I've got the 1981 telephone credit-card code. Do you?'"

A bell rang, signaling the end of the seminar. "I'm sorry, we're out of time," Dr. Marcus said. "Your assignment for next week is to think of anti-Reagan things to make and do. In the meantime," he added, turning up Country Joe and the Fish on the record player as the group filed out, "two, four, six, eight, organize and smash the state!"

Liquid Cash: An International Monetary Proviso

Why have certain countries grown into economic giants during the past 200 years? Why have others—some with far greater potential—become impoverished? What are the consequences of continuing this reckless economic policy?

Indeed, the answers to these life-and-death questions are not simple. One thing is entirely clear, however: The diplomats, secretaries of state, and concerned citizens who are busy trying to solve such fiduciary riddles have consistently and myopically overlooked the only deterrent to worldwide financial tragedy: global monetary reform.

Yes, the monetary systems of the world still largely reflect today's boundary-oriented societies whose jingoistic antecedents invented this divisively complicated form of exchange way back when kings minted their own coins and beheaded anyone who dared use currency with someone else's picture on it. Except for the lip service paid by world friendship assemblies and utopian newsletters to

the notion of a global monetary system, there has been
virtually no mass acknowledgment of the monetary chauvinism which so gravely impedes chances for world
survival. There have been no calls for reform within hallowed halls of governments. And worst of all, there have
been no calls for reform among those who continue to
suffer the most: financial columnists of many nations.

But a recent investigation has indicated that the population of the world is ready for drastic economic change. A
backstage minority such as the Benelux cartel should no
longer be able to tip the scales of European fiscal policy,
nor should the Sheik of Oman be permitted to float petro-
dollars onto the crap tables of Las Vegas. Clearly, the
world's pecuniary problems must be solved immediately.
To facilitate such sorely needed monetary reformation
and to smooth the bumpy roads of the inevitable global
village, a daring new international currency is hereby
presented. The new currency reflects in every aspect the
pan-hemispheric nature of life in today's shrinking world
and is so simple that even an illegal alien can use it to his
or her advantage.

The Global Currency differs from all known monetary
systems in several revolutionary ways. First and most important, it will be backed not by gold, silver, or other
precious metals, but the one substance on Earth that is
truly the most valuable to human beings: water.[1] Water is
the ideal base for a monetary system because its supply
is constant and therefore noninflationary. As long as there
are oceans, the people of the world will know for a fact
that the state of the exchequer is "solvent." (And don't
forget the vast unliquidated assets of the northern and
southern polar ice caps.) Since most countries have their

1. Salt, fresh, tap, and mineral water qualify. The government of
France, however, will not be permitted to manipulate world economy
by floating bottles of Perrier or Evian water.

own reserves of H_2O, there will be no need for wars concerning money—unless Saudi Arabia, for example, decided to take up arms against the more affluent Canal Zone. The cash-hoarding plutocracy will no longer exist, as even the most impoverished nations may make wise use of rain barrels to accumulate a large water reserve. With the advent of liquid cash, rich new meaning will accrue to such phrases as "sponging off relatives" and "drowning in riches"; meaningful new phraseology such as "Got any spare drops?" and "Sorry, I'm dry" will enter the language.

Second, the new currency will bear simple denominations describing measurable amounts of liquid. For example, one American cent will equal one drop Global. (A smaller denomination, the drip, will be minted for use in candy machines, subway turnstiles, and Tampax dispensers. Of course, the drip is intended primarily for those countries that have highways.) One hundred drops Global will equal one pint Global; two pints will equal one quart; four quarts will equal one gallon; four gallons will equal one jug. Denominations will also be available in multiples of ten, so that those countries reliant upon the decimal system may first familiarize themselves with the language of liquid while planning eventual disuse of the more complex monetary unit.[2] Under this new system, a tycoon will be tagged a "gallonaire."

Third, the new currency will actively promote ecology consciousness. The coins will be large and therefore easier to save, and they will be made of the recently discovered, inexpensive, nonlethal metal alloy, moron's silver.[3] The bills will remain the same convenient size as the American dollar, which seems to fit so smartly into the average Italian, Spanish, or Argentine wallet, and will be made of

2. Thus effectively phasing out the tedious metric system.
3. Due to excessive strip mining, the world is now experiencing a severe shortage of fool's gold.

paper recycled when the old money is confiscated. The bills will be green—the color citizens of the world turn when you have more of the stuff than they do.

And fourth, the design of the new currency will portray scenes of world history, thereby paying tribute to the traditions of all the world's inhabitants, from Ethiopians to Philadelphians. The planners of Global Currency have assembled a team of international artists and asked them to submit designs for our proposed new worldwide currency. What follows are the most significant renderings.

Man, mathematics, and masonry are the themes of this elaborate portrayal of dedicated Egyptians at work. Bill also instructs world population in history of the labor union, as pyramid builders are shown wearing the first hard hats.

Christopher Columbus would not have discovered red men if wild mastodons had not chased Indians across the Bering Strait in 10,000 B.C. Global currency salutes this fortuitous event, without which Americans would have no cause to celebrate Thanksgiving.

Hundreds of thousands of years ago, aliens from an advanced civilization visited Neanderthal man, transmitting knowledge of the universe which enabled residents of caves to construct astrological computers, design interplanetary airports, and teleport themselves from Mexican jungles to other galaxies.

This long-delayed coin commemorates publication of Mao Tse-tung's revolutionary thoughts. As the Chairman himself has said: "Unite and take part in banking and monetary activity to improve the economic and political status of the masses."

The tiny principate of Liechtenstein exists solely as a ski resort and tax shelter for international financiers. The ten-gallon bill symbolizes this unique duality, depicting a banker skiing to his vault.

*Earth's atmosphere has been the scene of many marvelous achieve-
ments. As man attempts to enlarge his universe, the skies have been
filled with all sorts of beings, including the three varieties shown
rocketing through space on the 20-gallon bill: a monkey, a woman,
and a Cuban.*

*The 50-drop coin portrays perhaps the most momentous occasion
of recorded history: Caligula's horse, flanked by his toga-clad peers,
filibustering before the Roman Senate.*

A defense-conscious America backs an unpopular government in a
Third World country teeming with the starved, seething with revo-
lution, and yearning to be free. The 100-drop coin celebrates the
ritual passage of power, as Uncle Sam presents a general in a
Panama hat with the first installment of a twenty-million-dollar aid
package.

A teeming, seething, yearning Third World country rises up against
the forces of imperialist America. The 75-drop coin depicts the
ritual taking of hostages as a revolutionary in a Panama hat explains the history of his struggle to a United Fruit executive.

The Last Survey

What is the last survey?

The last survey is exactly what it says it is: a final tabulation of the feelings, beliefs, and attitudes of all Americans in all age groups, income brackets, occupational divisions, and religious, racial, and ethnic categories.

Here at the Institute for How Americans Feel Most of the Time About Nearly Everything (IHAFMTANE), it was our goal to present a picture of the typical American definitive enough to preclude the necessity for any further poll or taking of the national pulse. Now that the results of The Last Survey have been tabulated, we have accomplished our goal, and we can all sit back, relax, and contemplate a poll-free future.

How was the survey taken?

To make our poll really definitive and comprehensive, we had to reach all Americans at any hour of the day or night about their thoughts on everything from the SALT talks to salt-free diets; nuclear proliferation to the nuclear family; jeans from France to laboratory genes. We wanted to reach "The New Right," "The New Consensus," "The New Narcissists," "The New Bisexuals," "The Old Left-Wing Coalition," "The Silent Majority," "Jews for Jesus,"

"Democrats for Nixon," "The Woodstock Nation," "The Iroquois Nation," the "disaffected," the "disenfranchised," and the "dyspeptic."

There was only one way to take The Last Survey. We had to "tap in" to our respondents, and thereby facilitate a kind of "perpetual poll." Through a complex system of nationwide canvassing, we found 5,000 volunteers willing to allow us to implant a tiny disk at the base of their skulls. Our questions were then relayed through a centrally located transmitter and received simultaneously by all 5,000 of the tiny brain implants. Without the respondent's even realizing that he or she was being questioned, his or her answers were automatically relayed back to our specially programmed computer. Thus, IHAFMTANE was able to conduct a round-the-clock poll without wasting so much as a second of anybody's valuable time. (And according to The Last Survey, there is widespread agreement among Americans that time is valuable.)[1]

We realize that this type of methodology might be perceived as strange. In fact, a poll of major American pollsters revealed that it was "highly unusual" (Gallup), "totally bizarre" (Harris). "completely devoid of credibility because there's no plus-or-minus factor" (Yankelovich), and "What the—?" (Roper). Nevertheless, for our purposes, it was entirely appropriate.

Tell us something about your percentages.

Okay. Sometimes they're listed, and sometimes when IHAFMTANE didn't feel like listing them, they're not. When the percentages *are* listed, however, they are all rounded off to the nearest tenth, except in certain cases, when they're not. Moreover, the reader will note that in some instances, the percentages total more than 100. As

1. But not as valuable as space.

we like to joke in the polling business, "that's the way the computer reads out."

You must have a lot of data that you haven't even had the time to decipher. What are you going to do with the remainder of The Last Survey?

Probably donate it to some sort of big brother agency, and write off the whole thing as a tax loss. On the other hand, we could use the reams and reams of complicated, double-digit columns that are cross-referenced eighteen different ways as insulation for the chic, downtown townhouse that we're renovating. Don't worry—IHAFMTANE will think of *something*.

Demographics

The family background of Americans presents ground for lively discussion. It breaks down this way: Thirty-eight percent of those surveyed state that their family "came over with the Rockefellers," while nearly one-quarter take pride in pointing out that their family "came over the same year as the Rockefellers." Moreover, one-tenth of our respondents agree with the statement "My cousin's brother-in-law works in a store and once sold a scarf to Happy Rockefeller."

Significantly, several respondents report that their family tried to "duplicate the Kon-Tiki adventure—no survivors," while only one revealed that his paternal grandfather fled the Cossacks, came over steerage, and today delivers stats to *Penthouse* magazine.

Many of those surveyed, however, claim to have Indian ancestors, tracing their roots all the way back to Princess

Summer Fall Winter Spring on the old "Howdy Doody Show."

Where Americans live (ranked in order of population density):

> Sun Belt: 28%
> Hog Belt: 18%
> Smog Belt: 15%
> Van Allen Belt: 14%
> Bible Belt: 14%
>   New Testament: 12%
>   Old Testament: 2%
> The Belt Parkway in Brooklyn: 14%
> The kind of loft Jill Clayburgh has in *It's My Turn*:
>   Women—13%
>   Men—1%
> Out of the trunk of my '57 Ford Fairlane: 11%
> In my mind, man: 8%
> Anywhere they have no-fault divorce: 5%

Occupation:

> Woman in gray flannel suit: 15%
> Man in gray flannel suit: 48%
> I make Sammy run: 12%
> Sammy: 32%
> Welfare cheat: 18%
> Racehorse tout: 5%
> Cheap thug: 8%

> I run the Three-Card Monte game in front of the Pussycat Theater: 10%
> Steal and sell airline discount coupons: 6%
> Shocked and dismayed—I'm an investigative reporter: 29%
> Making it all real—I'm a novelist: 25%
> Shocked, dismayed, and thinking about making it real—I'm an investigative reporter currently at work on a novel: 54%
> What difference does it make?—Does David Rockefeller work?: 90%

Income:

That's between me and my agent: 10%
Have you seen my agent?: 15%
More than Carmelita Pope but less than David Rockefeller:
90%
Enough to make monthly payments on my brand new Buick
Electra with the sky-blue interior, but not without taking a
third mortgage on my suburban split-level house with the
authentic Japanese rock garden: 35%
I owe everybody in town fifty bucks: 71%

I am—

Living alone: 10%
Living with a roommate: 15%
Harboring a fugitive: 3%
Married: 21%
Married but thinking about divorce: 11%
Divorced: 18%
Divorced but thinking about marriage: 11%
Wondering "what's it all about, Alfie?": 63%

Culture

The ten television personalities with the most integrity:

Walter Cronkite
Phil Donahue
Fury
Ed McMahon
Toni Tennille
Karen Valentine
Peggy Cass
David Soul
The guy who plays "Animal" on "Lou Grant"
Reverend Ike

More women than men agree with the statement "It's okay to wear white after Labor Day," while more men, across the board, express the belief that "White is only for weddings, and if the weddings occur after Labor Day, then I guess it's okay to wear white."

Percentagewise, more people joined the Cheese-of-the-Month Club than registered to vote, but fewer overall than those who instituted a chain letter.

Ninety-eight percent of the residents of Coeur D'Alene, Idaho, believe that the worst disaster within recent memory was the day Charles Kuralt drove through town without stopping. However, 84% believe that the worst disaster occurred the day Charles Kuralt stopped—and asked for gas.

(Women only) *My mother refers to balls of dust that you find on the floor as—*

> Dust bunnies: 75%
> Dust mice: 68%
> Dust kitties: 61%
> Stuff you wouldn't find in Happy Rockefeller's house: 90%

One hundred percent of the first-generation immigrant males surveyed identified George Washington as "a wide receiver in the NFL," whereas 66% of the population in general identified Arnold Schwarzenegger as "the prime minister of West Germany."

During the past year, nearly three-fourths of the over-65 female population have informed a person on the street that "Your zipper is down," "Your purse is open," or "Your hair is messed up."

There is nearly unanimous agreement that the worst Johnny Carson monologue was on April 21, 1969.

More Americans can identify their astrological sign than can name their blood type, but not nearly as many know their age in dog years.

When I think about my career, I—

Take a nap: 45%
Take drugs: 33%
Take something from a store: 19%
(East and West Coast only) Take a meeting: 75%

Ninety-eight percent of the women surveyed never burned their bras in the sixties. However, 57% scorched their underwear in a coin-operated dryer during the seventies.

For most people, the seventies really started in 1975, when Lester Maddox "went electric."

Preferences

Fifty-eight percent of those surveyed admitted that, while eating an Oreo cookie, they remove the top half first and then eat the filling.

How Americans prefer to fly:

No clouds: 85%
With an important team on board: 79%
Without people in turbans: 68%
Stand by: 51%
Still standing by: 51%
Astral projection: 35%
The way David Rockefeller does: 90%

The most popular foods among teenagers:

> Pizza
> Pizza in a tube
> Pizza in a box
> BBQ porkwich
> Fried grease
> The old man's Kahlua

Household features that Americans prefer most:

> Another Kitchen Magician
> A Barcalounger
> A fuck chair
> Another set of vases in graduated sizes
> Giant imitation toadstools for the lawn
> An octagonal bathtub with brasslike features
> A TV set that answers the phone
> A TV set that is also a kidney dialysis machine
> Whatever David Rockefeller has

What shut-ins would most like to hear on the radio:

> Easy listenin': 55%
> Top of the Pops: 42%
> The police band: 38%
> Big bands: 65%
> A talk show host who insults them: 88%
> A discussion about the Rockefellers: 90%

Who Americans would most want as a houseguest:

> Paul Lynde: 89%
> Betty Ford: 75%
> Not Jerry Ford: 95%
> Edsel Ford (but only if he comes by bus): 64%
> David Rockefeller (but only if he pays): 90%

Most Americans agree that Szechuan food tastes like Pine-Sol, while a minority is of the opinion that it is more reminiscent of Absorbine, Jr.

Sex

Among professional hostesses, the most frequently mentioned role models were Katy Winters, Kitty on "Maverick," and Della Street.

Who wears the pants in the family?

Men: 40%
Women: 35%
David Rockefeller: 90%
Don't have any pants: 13%
Pants are at the dry cleaners: 28%

Forty-nine percent of Americans have experienced "close encounters of the fourth kind," the code phrase for entering a spaceship from behind.

Thirteen percent of all Americans have had sex in a hot tub while watching reruns of "Quincy" on their Betamax.

Qualities college-age women prefer in men:

Smart
Considerate
Spiritual
Likes to cook—and willing to clean up immediately afterward
Respects elders
Trims cuticles
Laughs at my jokes
Changes toilet paper roll without being asked
Doesn't put his Cruex on my shelf
Does not now and never did own an ant farm
Does not speak Esperanto
Flosses regularly—but only in private

Wouldn't even think of asking me to swallow his you-know-what

Has the brains of Albert Einstein, the physique of Nick Nolte, the chin of Kirk Douglas, the hands of Michael Douglas, the presence of Mike Douglas, the dimples of John Davidson, the forehead crease of Robert Mitchum, the diction of Laurence Olivier, a wardrobe by Giorgio Armani, and a money belt by David Rockefeller

Qualities college-age men prefer in women:

Smart
Considerate
Spiritual
Knows how to cook—and doesn't make my eggs too runny
Laughs at my jokes
Has no moles on shoulders or face
Trims nostril hair
Realizes birth control is her responsibility but does not use a diaphragm
Does not leave used Tampax in my wastebasket
Better yet, does not have a period
Doesn't mind if I keep my Black and Decker drill in the living room
Has the brains of Jane Pauley, the body of Ursula Andress, the soul of Phyllis George, a throat like the Grand Canyon, and a lot of crotchless underwear

(Women) *When I have sex, I think about—*

My partner: 50%
My partner's partner: 33%
Whether or not I turned on the telephone answer machine: 82%
Whether or not I turned off the waffle iron: 45%
Whether or not I remembered to insert my diaphragm: 91%
The importance of regular dental checkups: 24%
What a good idea the Jews had with circumcision: 99%
Ferrante and Teicher: 0.3%

(Men) *When I have sex, I think about—*

My partner: 50%
My partner's best friend: 33%
My mother: 12%
How long I'll have to wait before calling sports hotline: 45%
How lucky I am that I'm not David Rockefeller: 90%
How much I wish I was David Rockefeller: 90%
The Dionne Quintuplets: 0.3%

Politics

In the 1960s, 18% of college-age women joined SDS in the mistaken belief that it was a sorority.

In the 1960s, 75% of college-age men joined SDS knowing that it was a fraternity.

To fight inflation, 12% of the upper class has removed Brie from their shopping lists, while 28% now stretch their supply with Brie-helper.

America should give foreign aid to oppressed people, but not if they—

Talk with their mouths full: 78%
Sing at the table: 70%
Don't iron their sheets: 68%

What does ERA stand for?

I think it has something to do with the laundry: 33%
A kind of missile the Russians have more of than we do: 54%
The monogram of Eleanor Roosevelt, with a typo: 25%
An evil plan of David Rockefeller's to get women to do all of his heavy lifting: 90%

Approximately two-thirds of the left-leaning political activists surveyed have had their pants tailored by Eldridge Cleaver.

Who's to blame for the Middle East situation?

> Jews: 68%
> Arabs: 71%
> Dark people who don't shave: 95%
> David Rockefeller and the Trilateral Commission: 90%
> The Boxing Commission: 11%
> The theory of entropy: 6%
> The law of supply and demand: 4%
> The free agency clause in Reggie Jackson's contract: 2%

Literacy

Seventy-three percent of those surveyed think R-O-L-A-I-D-S spells "relief."

Over half of all Americans do not know that the following are names of colors—or are, in fact, words:

> Putty
> Titian
> Puce
> Greige

Most Americans agree with the statement "It don't matter one way or t'other if youse says 'irregardless,' and anyone who say that it do, well, I don't pay him no nevermind."

When asked to say something in French, those Americans who have studied that particular foreign language for one semester replied, "Frère Jacques," while those who have visited France more than once but less than five times answered, "Ce soir?"

Seventy-five percent of those polled agree with the statement "Valvoline is the maid who cleans up at Indy 500," while nearly half identified Machu Picchu as a "tribe of Peruvian jocks."

Beliefs

The dice are loaded and the dealer works for the house.

> Agree: 43%
> Disagree: 38%
> Where are the dice?: 83%

The world is going to hell in a—

> Handbasket: 23%
> Briefcase: 32%
> Découpaged lunchbox: 14%
> Set of Vuitton luggage: 11%
> Chevy van: 73%

Cancer is caused by—

> Panty hose: 49%
> The promotion you're not going to get: 21%
> Your parents' tumors: 66%
> The frog you tortured in biology class: 37%
> All that paste you ate in second grade: 28%
> David Rockefeller: 90%
> Pods sent by the USSR: 61%

Ninety-two percent of Americans believe in God, while 87% believe that if there is a God, why doesn't He/She ever take them out to lunch?

The favorite dinnertime prayer among lapsed Catholics and stand-up Jesuits is "Rub-a-dub-dub, Thanks for the Grub, Yay God!"

> I believe in the concept of heaven and hell: 93%
> I believe that you make your heaven or hell here on Earth: 86%
> I believe that war is hell: 82%
> Pollsters should go to hell: 80%

More Jews feel guilty, most of the time, than Baptists, but fewer, overall, than Mormons or Shiite Muslims—none of whom suffer as much as Young Hegelians for Peace.

> Christmas is too commercial: 97%
> Christmas is not commercial enough: 13%
> I want more presents: 100%

Among lower-income respondents who have no hot water, can't pay the rent, and are having ketchup sandwiches for dinner, no one agreed with the statement "I'm poor, but at least I have my health."

While slightly over half of the homemakers surveyed agree with the statement "It's better to thicken gravy with arrowroot than with cornstarch," 33% would rather "go out and order gravy." However, among those who buy gravy in a can, there is widespread agreement that you have to "doctor the hell out of it."

Most women believe that "toxic shock syndrome" occurs when you wear tampons and polyester at the same time, whereas a large minority expresses the belief that if, while wearing a maxipad and Tris-treated pajamas simultaneously, you eat a T-bone steak covered with A.1. Sauce, the body instantly becomes a "toxic time bomb."

Most Americans believe that Perrier water is shipped in supertankers and bottled in Secaucus, New Jersey.

Forty-two percent of those surveyed adhere to the notion that Wuthering Heights is a suburb of Cleveland.

Nearly 90% of all Americans believe that "Writers are pulling the wool over my eyes, but not as much as David Rockefeller."

We need more—

> B-1 bombers: 51%
> Self-respect: 24%
> Money: 95%
> Dress shields: 87%

Significantly, one-third of those surveyed express the belief that the first female impersonator in America traversed the thirteen colonies, doing impressions of Dolley Madison, Mrs. James Monroe, and Judy Garland.

Most Americans have had the following psychic experiences (ranked in ascending order of frequency).

> Out-of-body
> Out-of-body-and-into-someone-else's
> Time travel
> Think I've time-traveled, but didn't have my watch
> ESP
> The feeling that you've already experienced what you're experiencing (*déja vu*)
> The feeling that you've already smelled what you're smelling (*déja pu*)
> The feeling that no matter what it is, you've seen it all— twice (*bored*)
> Visions of future in which I find large sums of unmarked bills
> Visions of David Rockefeller

If you have experienced time-travel, where have you gone?

> Tombs of the ancients: 13%
> Subterranean homes of tiny elves: 29%
> A more enlightened plane where everyone looks up to me: 74%
> My parents' house: 8%
> The refrigerator where Julia Child keeps her leftovers: 36%
> David Rockefeller's wallet: 90%
> Out for a beer: 44%

I believe in—

> Sasquatch: 12%
> The Loch Ness Monster: 19%
> The Bermuda Triangle: 23%
> The Symbionese Liberation Army: 3%
> The Christian Anti-Communist Crusade: 3%
> Megan Marshack: 90%
> The Pointer Sisters: 41%

While 100% of Americans living in rural areas have been visited or expect to be visited by aliens, fewer than nine-tenths of those on the corner of 125th Street and Seventh Avenue claim to have sold dope to aliens. However, 65% of those living in suburbs have booked a seat on the first commercial flight to the moon.

In my previous life I was—

> A sorcerer
> A gaffer
> The guy who sat behind Rudolph Valentino in homeroom
> Robin Hood's press agent
> Nelson Rockefeller
> The inventor of the petri dish
> Born in a petri dish
> The Oracle of Delphi

A fresco repairman
Popcorn concessionaire at the chariot races
A camp follower
Tourist at Stonehenge
Fishwife
Midwife
Housewife
Yma Sumac
Still am Yma Sumac
Don't know what I am now

If tuna is the "chicken of the sea," then quail is the "tuna of the land."

Agree: 64%
Disagree: 18%
Not hungry right now: 38%

Sports and Recreation

Fifty-seven percent of the self-identified "baseball fans" are still discussing the triple play call in the 1980 Houston-Philadelphia playoffs, and two-thirds are convinced that if you take the number of letters in Carl Yasztrzemski's name, multiply by Mickey Mantle's lifetime RBI record, and divide by Pete Rose's salary, you get the combination to David Rockefeller's safe-deposit box.

Seventy-five percent of football players report that they take drugs to heighten, not lessen, the pain.

The most frequently used opening chess play is "The Fools' Gambit" (1 QRP-R3).

I feel that sports—

> Are institutionalized violence: 22%
> Are mindless: 17%
> Are good training for life: 38%
> Are fun: 77%
> Are owned by David Rockefeller: 90%

Among New York Yankee fans, there is unanimous agreement with the statement, "Boston sucks."

I go to my local stadium—

> Whenever the home team is in town: 56%
> Occasionally: 44%
> Whenever there's ten-cent beer night: 92%
> To see the Grateful Dead: 88%
> To get rowdy and punch someone in the face: 95%

Most popular card games (ranked in order of popularity):

> Old Maid
> Fish
> Crazy Eights
> War
> Authors
> Poker (but only if I supply the deck)

While many Americans are content watching slow-motion ski-jump replays on "Wide World of Sports," a significant majority would like to see someone knock a battery off Robert Conrad's shoulder.

(Women) Without sports men would—

> Have nothing to talk about: 98%
> Eat less: 75%
> Get into something else, like the weather: 28%
> Kill each other: 67%
> Probably die: 96%

Most Americans surveyed agree with the statement "Basketball coaches should lighten up and stop wearing suits," although, when it comes to football, the exact same percentage endorses the statement "It's okay if Tom Landry never smiles."

Hockey players should—

> Not be allowed to remove their gloves: 25%
> Wear gloves with pointy metal studs: 31%
> Carry handguns: 46%
> Take their clothes off and skate naked: 85%

Drugs

Three-fourths of the doctors surveyed feel that the regular smoking of marijuana leads to such dangerous practices as guzzling Pabst Blue Ribbon beer, mainlining Fizzies, snorting the filling inside Mars Bars, and taking nationwide surveys.

Thirty-two percent of those surveyed agree that "a Tequila Sunrise is something you only see at Puerto Vallarta," while a full two-thirds believes that angostura bitters is a controlled substance in Delaware.

Frank Sinatra, Dean Martin, Sammy Davis, Jr., and other members of the legendary "Rat Pack" had a lot of fun when they got drunk together at Las Vegas hotels.

> Agree: 18%
> Disagree: 82%

Ninety-one percent of the coke freaks surveyed have known or heard of at least one other coke freak who has died rapping.

According to The Last Survey, the Ziploc bag has never been used for a sandwich.

While 75% of Americans believe that "The entire economy of Bhutan is based on the smuggling of Lavoris," there is unanimous agreement that the Lavoris Company owns Bhutan—which is thought to be owned by David Rockefeller.

Twelve percent of people who saw God while on LSD in the sixties now claim to have religious experiences after drinking a hot, buttered Nyquil.

Personal Condition

I have a—

> Headache: 29%
> Stomach ache: 31%
> Toothache: 10%
> Painful ache at the base of my skull: 100%
> I'm not feeling too well in general, but even all that money couldn't save Nelson Rockefeller: 90%

Some Final Comments on The Last Survey

Should you disagree with the findings of The Last Survey, you'll simply have to keep it to yourself. If you agree with our results, however, feel free to drop the Institute for How Americans Feel Most of the Time About Nearly Everything a line. And, to those survey volunteers who have been complaining that the tiny perpetual-polling brain implants have been causing painful headaches, well, we'll be monitoring your condition, and if it worsens during your sleep, for example, the Institute for How Americans Feel Most of the Time About Nearly Everything will be the first to know about it.